Surrey

A DOG WALKER'S GUIDE

Jane Eyles

COUNTRYSIDE BOOKS
NEWBURY BERKSHIRE

First published 2012
© Jane Eyles 2012
Reprinted 2015
Revised and reprinted 2017

All rights reserved. No reproduction
permitted without the prior permission
of the publisher:

COUNTRYSIDE BOOKS
3 Catherine Road
Newbury, Berkshire

To view our complete range of books,
please visit us at
www.countrysidebooks.co.uk

ISBN 978 1 84674 281 1

Cover picture supplied by
Roger Evans

Designed by Peter Davies, Nautilus Design
Produced through The Letterworks Ltd., Reading
Typeset by KT Designs, St Helens
Printed by The Holywell Press, Oxford

Contents

Walk

Appendix

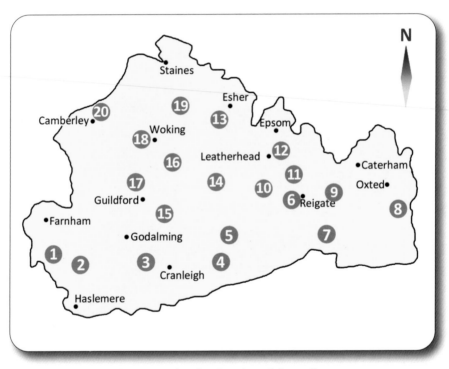

Area map showing location of the walks.

INTRODUCTION

A friend once said to me that a walk is not a walk if you haven't got the back of a dog in front of you; she was right. A dog keeps you company, gives you someone to talk to and allows you to open conversations with complete strangers that in time become close friends. A walk with a dog should be a pleasure, lowering your stress levels and keeping you healthy. However, over the years, like many dog owners, I had fallen into the trap of walking round the same fields day after day, because it was easy; I knew the route and therefore felt safe. What I was missing out on was the fantastic scenery, history and diverse landscapes that our county offers. So, this guide was born.

This book has done all the hard work for the dog walker: it allows you to go on a walk without the worry that you are going to meet a dead-end, or a stile that your dog can't cross. These walks are all dog-friendly and my dogs, Benson, a golden retriever, and Meg, a brown RSPCA rescue, have personally tested them all. Our requirements for a good dog walk were:

- An interesting landscape, with varied views and points of interest along the way.
- Somewhere safe to park.
- Safe, free running space for the dogs to enjoy hunting and running and to meet other dogs.
- Dog-friendly pubs, restaurants and cafés along the way.
- Minimum road walking, although this is difficult in our ever congested society.
- Easy-to-follow circular routes.
- Minimal exposure to livestock.
- Safe dog swimming or dipping water.

The majority of the walks are stile free, although a couple do cross fields where stiles are a necessity; in this case they are all easily accessible by dogs with lift-up dog gates or can be bypassed through hedges or gates. The walks that go over farmland can, of course, sometimes contain livestock and care should be taken when walking across these fields. Please take note of the Countryside Code overleaf. As a couple of the walks also cover areas of horse ownership, be aware that you may well meet horses on the bridleways.

Surrey is a county of many differing landscapes, split down the middle by the Surrey Hills, an Area of Outstanding Natural Beauty, along which snakes the old Pilgrims' Way and from which you can see for miles. To the north the River Wey feeds into the Thames and has created some lovely meadows, as well as the timeless beauty of the Wey Navigation Canal. Across the county large areas of heathland are preserved and offer protected habitats for wildlife, which without them might not be able to survive. To the south of the county you find the picturesque Surrey villages that nestle in valleys beside hills and rivers with ancient churches and lovely country pubs overlooking cricket greens. From this myriad of destinations, these walks have been created. In the majority of cases a country pub is included either at the start or halfway round the walk. If you are planning to have a meal, do call to make a reservation in advance, and let them know you will be with dogs, in this way they can make sure you have a table in the right place.

Happy walkies!

Jane Eyles

. . . .

PUBLISHER'S NOTE

We hope that you obtain considerable enjoyment from this book; great care has been taken in its preparation. Although at the time of publication all routes followed public rights of way or permitted paths, diversion orders can be made and permissions withdrawn.

We cannot, of course, be held responsible for such diversion orders and any inaccuracies in the text which result from these or any other changes to the routes nor any damage which might result from walkers trespassing on private property. We are anxious though that all details covering the walks are kept up to date and would therefore welcome information from readers which would be relevant to future editions.

The simple sketch maps that accompany the walks in this book are based on notes made by the author whilst checking out the routes on the ground. They are designed to show you how to reach the start, to point out the main features of the overall circuit and they contain a progression of numbers that relate to the paragraphs of the text.

However, for the benefit of a proper map, we do recommend that you purchase the relevant Ordnance Survey sheet covering your walk. The Ordnance Survey maps are widely available, especially through booksellers and local newsagents.

ADVICE FOR DOG WALKERS

'The countryside is a great place to exercise dogs, but it's every owner's duty to make sure their dog is not a danger or nuisance to farm animals, wildlife or other people.' *(Excerpt from Natural England's Countryside Code. For further information go to www.naturalengland.co.uk)*

The Dog Walker's Code

To ensure that access to the countryside to people with dogs is a continued freedom, please make sure you follow the steps outlined below to protect the environment and demonstrate that you are a responsible dog owner:

■ By law, you must control your dog so that it does not disturb or scare farm animals or wildlife. I have tried to indicate in this book where you might come across animals. You do not have to put your dog on a lead on public paths, as long as it is under close control. But as a general rule, keep your dog on a lead if you cannot rely on its obedience. By law, farmers are entitled to destroy a dog that injures or worries their animals. A long lead is always a good investment.

■ If a farm animal chases you and your dog, it is safer to let your dog off the lead – don't risk getting hurt by trying to protect it.

■ Take particular care that your dog doesn't scare sheep and lambs or wander where it might disturb birds that nest on the ground and other wildlife – eggs and young will soon die without protection from their parents. As some of these walks cross areas known for their ground nesting birds, please be aware and watch out for warning signs that will indicate nesting areas.

■ Everyone knows how unpleasant dog mess is and it can cause infections – so always clean up after your dog. Also make sure your dog is wormed regularly to protect it, other animals and people. Do not leave bags of dog mess hanging on fences; if there is not a bin, take it with you and dispose of it responsibly.

■ At certain times, dogs may not be allowed on some areas of access land or may need to be kept on a lead. Please follow any signs.

■ Please make sure that your dog is wearing a collar and identity tag. This is for your own peace of mind, particularly if you are walking in a strange area, as it will help you be reunited if you become parted.

■ As many of these walks cover popular recreation areas, please be aware that not everyone likes dogs, and in fact some children can be scared of them. Please keep your dogs under control when there are other people around.

1

Tilford & Frensham Little Pond

The beach at Frensham Little Pond.

This walks starts and finishes at Tilford – a quintessential 'chocolate box' village south of Farnham, with a cricket green overlooked by a pub, a pretty stream and two medieval bridges. It takes you through woods along the River Wey to Frensham Common and ponds, looping around the Little Pond in one of the largest expanses of Surrey heathland in the county; a designated Site of Special Scientific Interest and special protection area. Owned and managed by the National Trust, the Little Pond provides important habitats for both plants and birds and on a fine day there is nothing better than a walk round this superb nature reserve.

Dogs can enjoy the freedom of running through woodland along the river bank on the way to and from the pond, and as the pond is such a popular dog

Dog factors

Distance: 5 miles.
Road walking: Crossing the road at Tilford green and again at Little Pond; 100 metres of quiet lane to and from the pond.
Livestock: You walk through a farm with pigs running free in the woods, although the path is well fenced.
Stiles: None.
Nearest vets: Elstead Veterinary Surgery, Elstead.

walking area, they have a wonderful time making new friends and exploring all the scents. Do be aware that certain areas of the pond may be fenced off to protect the birds.

Terrain
A gentle incline uphill to the pond through woods, on footpaths and sandy tracks. Around the pond the path is mainly sand.

Where to park
Park in Tilford Village Green car park on the left in front of the Barley Mow pub. **OS map:** Explorer 145 (GR SU 873434).

How to get there
Tilford lies south of the B3001 between Farnham and the A3 south of Godalming. Approaching from the A3, take the Milford turning and then the B3001. Pass through Elstead and turn left down Tilford Street after 2½ miles. The village is a mile down this road.

Nearest refreshments
The **Barley Mow** in Tilford serves good pub food and has a garden running down to the river. In summer you can sit outside and enjoy the cricket on the green. ☎ 01252 792205; www.thebarleymowtilford.com

Alternatively, take a picnic and sit and enjoy the sights at Frensham Little Pond at one of the many rest areas along its banks.

The Walk

1 With your back to the car park, walk across the green to the far right-hand corner. Cross the second road and the footpath can be found to the left of **The**

Surrey – A Dog Walker's Guide

Malt House on the corner. Follow the footpath through between the houses and it will bring you out onto the bank of the **River Wey**. Follow this path through the woods along the river, past a dog swimming area, until you reach a gateway, pass through the gate and up onto a quiet lane.

2 Turn right onto the lane and walk past a few houses on the right until after

Taking a dip in Frensham Little Pond.

about 100 metres you reach a smallholding. Pass through a metal sheep gate straight ahead of you onto a fenced path between the fields. Follow this path.

3 At the kissing gate turn right onto the bridleway and continue on this path through the woods, crossing a wooden bridge over a ford until you reach a path crossroads and you can see the road about 75 metres ahead of you. Turn left here and after 50 metres you reach the road.

4 Cross the road and bear left along the edge of the road for about 50 metres until you come to the footpath at the side of **Little Pond** on your right. Join this footpath and keep following it around the pond, keeping the pond on your right-hand side. As you walk round there are many areas to sit and enjoy the wildlife, while your dogs enjoy the water.

5 As you reach the top of the pond and re-enter some woods, take the main footpath to your right and walk over a boardwalk around the marshy area. On exiting this, turn right back towards the pond and pick up the main circular footpath again. This path crosses an area of **Frensham Common** that has been destroyed by fire and you can see the regeneration of the habitat. Follow this path along the edge of the pond, turning right at every junction until you re-enter the pine woods at the road end of the pond.

6 Cross the road, and retrace your steps back through the woods to **Tilford**.

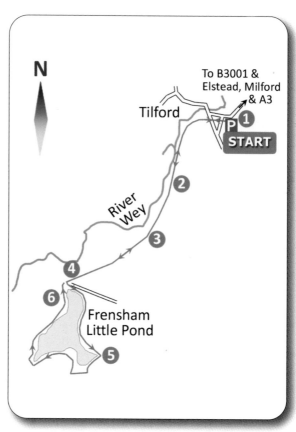

2

Thursley

Benson waiting on the boardwalk.

This walk takes you across Thursley Common to the Three Horseshoes, a dog-friendly pub famous for being saved from closing by being bought by the villagers. The pretty village of Thursley, where the architect Sir Edwin Lutyens was brought up and apparently had his first commission, sits just south of Thursley Common Nature Reserve. This is one of the largest remaining areas of Surrey heath and it includes areas of lowland heath, mire, wet heath and woodland. You will come across bog pools, sphagnum lawns and tracts of sandy soil. As large tracts of the reserve were destroyed by fire a few years ago you will be able to see Nature's wonderful skill of regeneration at work.

Other than some road walking to the pub, dogs can enjoy a completely free running walk across the common and through trees. You will pass a large pond with a good dog dipping area and as you reach the lower areas, and walk along the boardwalks, the dogs can enjoy mud and water – what more do they need?

Terrain
The majority of the walk is on sandy bridlepaths; however, the path to the village is uphill and quite narrow. Across the boardwalks, you do need to be careful that your dog stays with you if it can't swim; off the boardwalks the ground can be covered in water.

Where to park
The Moat car park. **OS map:** Explorer 145, with the section in Thursley village on Explorer 133 (GR SU 899416).

How to get there
Thursley lies south of the B3001 between Farnham and the A3 south of Godalming. Approaching from the A3, take the Milford turning and then the B3001. At Elstead village green, turn left. The moat car park is just over 1 mile on the left.

Nearest refreshments
The **Three Horseshoes** in Thursley. Dogs are allowed in the bar. Good quality pub food is served, with a daily changing menu, real ales and wines. If you want to eat in the bar, booking is recommended. ☎ 01252 703268; www.threehorseshoesthursley.com

The Walk
• •

❶ From the car park, facing the moat pond, take the footpath to your left around the pond, ignoring the wide bridlepath past the gate. After 50 metres, turn left at the junction. This brings you out of the pine trees and onto a wide sandy bridleway with an information board in front of you. Turn right.

Dog factors
• •

Distance: 4 miles.
Road walking: 100 metres to and from the pub.
Livestock: None.
Stiles: None.
Nearest vets: Elstead Veterinary Surgery, Elstead.

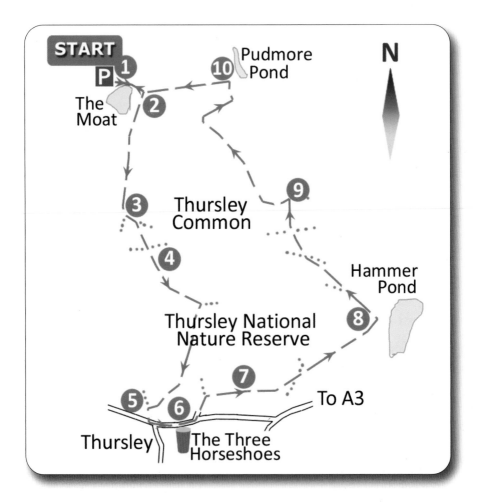

2 Follow this bridleway all the way up the nature reserve. On your left you will see evidence of the devastating fire that raged across the common in 2004. After 200 metres, just after a thicket of pine trees, the path branches; take the left-hand branch.

3 After 100 metres, cross straight over a wide bridlepath and start walking uphill. This brings you into some silver birch woods, and the path is sunk between two banks. At the next junction, keep left and you will see a field in front of you. Keep left and ignore the bridlepath to the right and keep on the footpath towards the right past the bridleway.

Near the end of the route.

4 Follow this path across the edge of a bank that looks down over the bridleway to the right as it leads through the edge of the woods. As you come down into some mature oaks in a dip, take the footpath straight ahead onto a sunken pathway between two high banks. This narrow path takes you uphill with banks either side of you. Cross straight over the path at the top of the hill.

5 You exit into **Thursley village** between some houses. Turn right to the road, and then left to walk up to the **Three Horseshoes**, which is 100 metres up the road on your right.

6 On leaving the pub, turn right and after 50 metres, take the footpath between two houses. Walk down and turn right onto the main sandy footpath. Follow this path all the way along, behind the back of the houses, until it reaches the end of the houses and bears right.

7 Turn left on this corner onto a narrow footpath through the gorse and heather; this takes you across the top of a hill. As you reach another wide bridlepath, turn left. From this point you get a fantastic view of the whole common. After 50 metres, take the right-hand bridleway. This path takes you downhill, through some heather towards some silver birch and pine trees at the bottom.

8 When you reach the bottom, straight ahead of you is **Hammer Pond** where the last iron forge in Surrey was built in 1610. Carry on straight ahead over two sandy paths and a large stone step to reach the pond and allow your dogs to have a swim and do a bit of water bird watching. To continue, retrace your steps to the second sandy path. Turn right onto it (left if you have not visited the pond) and follow it all the way along, ignoring any side paths. Cross straight over a major junction to head downhill.

9 At the bottom of the hill as the path bears to the right, you will see a black waymarker post that is a nature trail waymarker. Turn left here down a narrow sandy path and follow this path through the heather. You will reach the first boardwalk; take this across the bog and 200 metres after the black nature trail waymarker you will see another black nature trail waymarker. Turn right and follow the path to the next waymarker. Turn right here onto another set of boardwalks. After another short walk between boardwalks, you will see an information board on your left displaying the types of dragonflies that you can see. Keep straight on to the boardwalk.

10 At the T-junction turn left and the path will take you straight back to the information board at point 2.

Hascombe Hill

Benson admires the view towards Dunsfold.

Hascombe is a pretty Surrey village south of Godalming, in an Area of Outstanding Natural Beauty, comprising a cluster of houses, St Peter's church, which was rebuilt in the mid 19th century and was described by Sir John Betjeman as 'a Tractarian work of art', a village pond and the White Horse pub. It sits at the bottom of Hascombe Hill, the site of a ruined hill fort built by ancient Britons.

This lovely circular walk, which starts and finishes at the White Horse, gives you great views of the Surrey countryside to the south over Dunsfold airfield where the T.V. programme *Top Gear* is filmed. Dogs can run free for the whole of the route through the woodland and if you are lucky you might see a herd of deer roaming across the top of the hill.

Dog factors

Distance: 2½ miles.
Road walking: 50 metres around the village green at the end of the walk, back to the pub.
Livestock: There may be horses in fields on the left as you walk down the hill.
Stiles: None.
Nearest vets: Yew Tree Veterinary Centre, Cranleigh.

Terrain

Through the woods the path can get muddy. Watch out for tree roots and stones under the leaves. There is quite a steep climb up the hill at the beginning.

Where to park

There is a public car park opposite the White Horse. **OS map:** Explorer 134 (GR TQ 001394).

How to get there

Hascombe lies on the B2130 between Godalming and Cranleigh. From the A281 Guildford to Horsham road take the B2130 towards Dunsfold. Continue on this road, passing the turning to Dunsfold and bearing right to Hascombe. Keep straight on through the village and the pub is on your right.

Nearest refreshments

The **White Horse** in Hascombe serves good seasonal food, including local game. Well-behaved dogs are allowed in the public bar and garden. ☎ 01483 208258; www.whitehorsepub.net

The Walk

1 From the car park, cross the road and take the lane to the right of the pub as you face it, **Nore Lane**. After 100 metres turn right into the driveway of **Hascombe Place Farmhouse** and take the footpath to the left of the garage; this leads you up along a sunken pathway into the woods.

2 After 100 metres, at the waymarker sign, turn left uphill. After 50 metres this joins a wide track that comes in from the right. Follow this path up the hill.

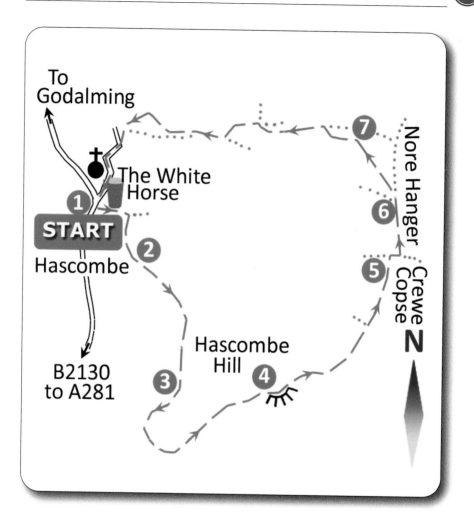

You will have a valley on your right-hand side and it will be a steady climb up the hill. As the path flattens out at the brow of the hill, turn right at the waymarker sign onto a narrower path through some cleared woodland below you.

❸ At the T-junction at the end of the cleared woodland, turn right through some rhododendrons. Follow this path as it winds all the way round the edge of the hill. You will have fantastic views to your right. To your left up the hill are the remains of the hilltop fort. You will eventually reach a cleared area with a tree trunk seat up a bank to your left. Take a while to sit and enjoy the view with **Dunsfold aerodrome** to the south.

4 Continue on the path from the seat and after 400 metres as you exit the pine trees, the path branches into two. Take the left-hand path, ignoring the right-hand path that would take you downhill. Pass an old metal fence and keep right as the path goes downhill towards the fields.

5 At the bottom of the hill pass through the wooden barriers and turn right up a sunken path, and then left at the coppiced wood. Keep straight on and you will see fields on your left and woods on your right. This is a good area for game birds.

6 After 300 metres, ignore the bridleway sign and turn left at the signed footpath, keeping on the footpath as it is drier.

7 As you reach the end of the hill, turn left at the next waymarker sign onto a footpath that winds gently downhill through trees, between the fields, and takes you all the way back down to the village. Walk round the village pond, past **St Peter's church** and the churchyard, and continue down **Church Lane** to reach the pub on the left, with your car park opposite.

Walliswood & Okewood

In the woods.

Walliswood is a small village to the far south of the county, almost on the Sussex border. To one side of the village is the Wallis Wood Nature Reserve, which is managed by the Surrey Wildlife Trust, whilst the rest of the area is surrounded by rolling countryside and criss-crossed with footpaths and bridleways. This walk takes you to the historic St John the Baptist church at Okewood, delightfully tucked away in the woods, then past the nature reserve, across fields and through some pretty clusters of houses.

The route starts and finishes at the Scarlett Arms pub in the village and for dogs it offers plenty of variety as it sets off in the woods, which are popular with other dog walkers, crosses loads of streams for swimming and cooling off, and open fields for running and rabbiting.

Terrain
Through the woods the path can get slippery, also the footpaths across the fields, depending on the time of year and weather. The bridlepaths are well maintained.

Where to park
There is a public car park opposite the Scarlett Arms at Walliswood. **OS map:** Explorer 134 (GR TQ 119381).

How to get there
Walliswood is west of the A29 between Dorking and Billingshurst. Some 1½ miles south of Ockley, turn off for Okewood Hill. Follow this road round to the right at the next junction and then turn right at the T-junction to reach Walliswood. The car park is on your left after you pass Froggetts Lane.

Nearest refreshments
The **Scarlett Arms** serves a range of pub food, with Malaysian specialities. Dogs are welcome on leads. Not open on a Monday lunchtime. ☎ 01306 627243; www.scarlettarms.co.uk

The Walk
• •

1 Facing the **Scarlett Arms**, cross the road and take the footpath 50 metres to the right of the pub after the bus shelter. This leads down a fenced path between houses and into the woods. After 100 metres you reach a fingerpost and a crossroads in the path. Continue straight on along this path through the woods.

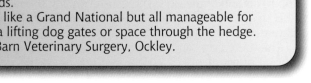

Dog factors
• •
Distance: 4¼ miles.
Road walking: 250 metres.
Livestock: You could meet horses on the bridleways. There may be sheep in two fields.
Stiles: 13. It sounds like a Grand National but all manageable for dogs, with access via lifting dog gates or space through the hedge.
Nearest vets: Ash Barn Veterinary Surgery, Ockley.

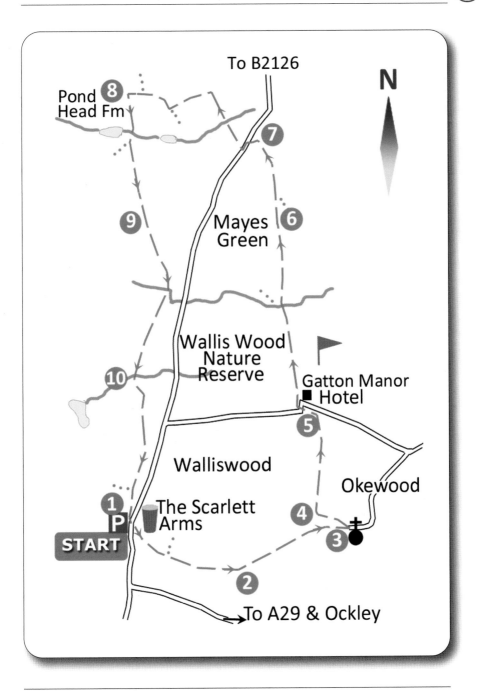

To B2126

N

Pond Head Fm 8

7

9

Mayes Green 6

Wallis Wood Nature Reserve

Gatton Manor Hotel

5

10

Walliswood

Okewood

The Scarlett Arms

1 P

START

4

3

2

To A29 & Ockley

2 After 500 metres, at a crossroads with some metal gates on your right, take the left-hand branch of the path; this takes you down through the woods with a wooden fence on your right. As you continue you will have a valley on your right-hand side. Continue down through the woods and, after 500 metres, the path winds down to the right into the valley and over a small wooden bridge. Up ahead of you is **Okewood church**, which can be reached via some steps.

3 If you don't want to visit the church, turn left after crossing the first bridge, over a second wooden bridge, so that you are crossing the small stream onto the other side of the valley. This path leads you along the side of the valley with the stream on your right-hand side.

4 After 200 metres bear right up a steep bank over a stile into a field. Keep straight ahead with the fence on your left-hand side. At the end of the field cross a second stile and beware of geese and turkeys in a fenced-off area on your right. Pass a house with a wide holly hedge on your right and bear right at the end of the hedge and then left, keeping on the footpath over a bridge and heading back into the woods.

5 After 200 metres you meet a quiet lane opposite the entrance to **Gatton Manor Hotel**. Turn left onto this lane – there is a wide grass verge – and after 75 metres turn right down **Trap Lane**, following the public bridleway sign. This is a narrow lane that passes some houses and after 100 metres turns to an unmade-up bridleway. Keep straight ahead, following this path through the woods, with **Gatton Manor Golf Course** on your right and **Wallis Wood Nature Reserve** on your left-hand side.

6 At the next big junction, ignore the left and right wide tracks and take the footpath straight ahead through a wooden gate into a field. Cross the next two fields over a couple of stiles to reach a road.

7 Cross the road and walk left uphill for 50 metres before going right over another stile into a field. At the end of the field go down a dip, over a bridge and a stream and back up into another field. When you reach the next hedge, turn left and walk along the hedge to the next stile into a field (which may have sheep in it). Cross the next two fields and you will come out onto a lane.

8 Turn left downhill past **Pond Head Farm** and the pond and then take the public footpath sign on the left into a field. Cross this field uphill to the top left of the hill and cross another stile into a lane.

9 Opposite you is a house called **Woodlands** – take the footpath to the left of their gate. Go over another couple of stiles through some fields until you reach a gate. Pass straight through this to some coppiced woodland, past some old animal shelters, and over another stile into another field. Cross this field on the diagonal, and go over another stile, following the edge of the field along some woodland on your right. At the end of the field cross a final stile into the woods.

10 Bear left after 20 metres and then right down an avenue of pine trees. After 200 metres you will see a thatched house on your left and a barn on your right. Cross straight over the gravel driveway and through the wooden gate. Keep straight on the grass track, across another gravel drive, taking the footpath between the houses. At the end of the path turn left onto the village green and the **Scarlett Arms** is down the road on your right.

Crossing the fields at Walliswood.

Friday Street & Leith Hill

The steep 'root' down from Leith Hill tower.

Leith Hill is Surrey's highest point and it is said that on a good day you can see as far as London in the north and the English Channel in the south. Now owned by the National Trust the wooded hill is criss-crossed with footpaths up to the tower, which sits at its peak, and is a simply fantastic area for dogs. The walk is worth it for the view alone, and there are masses of tables at the summit, so why not make a day of it and take a picnic? As the climb to the tower is very steep from the south, this route starts in the small hamlet of Friday Street to the north of the hill, a cluster of houses around an old mill pond, and where the popular Stephan Langton Inn is found. The route up to the tower from here is on wide bridlepaths and is a steady gentle climb.

For dogs, there are masses of woods, bracken and undergrowth in which to go off hunting, and the mill pond at Friday Street is safe for a dog dip.

Terrain

The footpath up the hill is quite rough and stony, and can get muddy in places. However, there is always a diversion around muddy areas. From the top of the hill down, the path is mainly sandy and on some unmade roads.

Where to park

The Friday Street National Trust car park. **OS map:** Explorer 146 (GR TQ 126457).

How to get there

From the A25 between Dorking and Gomshall, turn off southwards at Manor Farm, just west of Wotton, signposted to Friday Street. After 1 mile (just after the turning to Abinger Common on your right) take a very sharp left turn (almost back on yourself), signposted to Friday Street. The car park is on your right after 1 mile.

Nearest refreshments

The **Stephan Langton** pub in Friday Street serves a selection of à la carte dishes, daily changing specials and baguettes. Not open on a Monday. Dogs are allowed in the bar area. ☎ 01306 730775; www.stephanlangton.pub

Leith Hill Tower houses an information room and servery at weekends, plus Wednesdays and Fridays from April to October, but check the opening times as they do vary. ☎ 01306 712711; www.nationaltrust.org.uk

The Walk

· ·

1 From the car park, take the footpath downhill adjacent to the road. After 100 metres go down a few steps and then turn left and right onto the road. At the bottom of the hill turn right in front of the mill pond, following the signs to the **Stephan Langton**.

2 Follow this road up past the inn, which is on your left-hand side, and after 50 metres the road ends. Pass through a barrier onto a bridleway into the woods. Follow this wide bridleway up through the valley, ignoring any footpaths to the left or right. Just after a wooden bridge on your left-hand side you will see a house on your right and after 50 metres you will come out onto a quiet lane.

Surrey – A Dog Walker's Guide

Dog factors

Distance: 5 miles.
Road walking: 200 metres from the car park past the pub and back to the car park again.
Livestock: You could meet horses on the bridleways.
Stiles: None.
Nearest vets: Ash Barn Veterinary Surgery, Ockley.

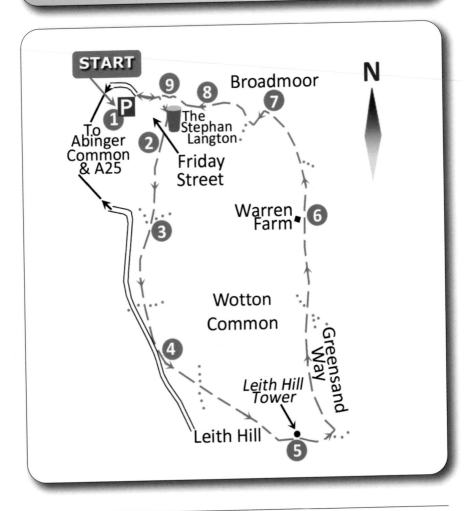

❸ Turn left onto the road and after 50 metres take the right-hand fork, signposted as a public bridleway. This path takes you up through the woods and you will come across an area of woodland that has been cleared on your left-hand side. Keep straight on, ignoring any footpath signs, and re-enter the woods at the end of the cleared area. After 200 metres bear right as the path branches, and you will reach a driveway to a house. Cross straight over, with the house on your left-hand side. After another 50 metres you reach **Leith Hill Road**.

❹ Turn left onto this road (there is a safe verge to walk along) and after 50 metres at a road junction cross over the junction to the bridleway sign. Enter the woods here. After 500 metres go straight on at a footpath crossroads and after another 500 metres carry straight on at another footpath crossroads. And after another 50 metres ignore left and right paths, keeping straight on. After 400 metres as you reach the brow of the hill and a slight clearing in the woods, the main footpath bears round to the right. Follow this path for 50 metres as it leads down through some pine trees and bears round to the left, with a mountain biking, sandy jump area on your left in the trees. As you leave this behind you, after another 50 metres, the path bears right and, after another 50 metres, you should see **Leith Hill Tower** straight ahead of you. Head towards the tower.

❺ After admiring the view and with your back to the tower, facing south, take the left-hand path down from the tower and descend this steep path for about 200 metres, watching out for tree roots, until you reach a large footpath crossway. Take the left-hand bridlepath, signposted 'The Greensand Way'. This wide path leads down through woods and bracken at a gentle incline. After about 1,500 metres, ignore footpath signs left and right and keep straight on.

❻ At the bottom of the hill, join a tarmac driveway to a house and stableyard (**Warren Farm**). Turn left down the unmade roadway. Follow this roadway, ignoring any turnings off.

❼ At the T-junction at the end of the private road, turn left onto a very quiet road, with some pretty cottages on your right-hand side. After 50 metres, just past **Leith Cottage**, take the footpath on your right past the parish noticeboard. This leads you up between the houses. At the end of the houses, take the right-hand footpath. After another 50 metres, at the waymarker, take the left-hand footpath up a narrow, steep path between holly bushes. Follow this path, crossing a small road, and then after 50 metres another road.

'King of the castle' at Leith Hill.

8 On the other side of this road, take the path signposted through the **Wotton Estate** (there is a big 'Private Property' sign at the entrance to the path), which is about 20 metres to the right down the road. Take this path down through the woods, ignoring the National Trust path on the left-hand side – keep heading downhill.

9 At the bottom of the hill, exit the woods by the far side of the mill pond at **Friday Street**. Walk 50 metres along the road with the mill pond on your left. Turn left to walk back up to the **Stephan Langton**, or carry straight on up the hill to the car park.

6

Reigate Heath

Looking out for golfers.

Reigate is a lovely old market town, with a great selection of shops and restaurants, at the foot of Reigate Hill. This is a gentle walk across the lowland heath, grassland and alder woods of Reigate Heath to the west of the town, which also takes in a loop across some grassland, fields and a river. Part of the heath is a golf course and the paths run adjacent to some of the fairways. At the clubhouse is Reigate Heath windmill, the bottom of which has been converted into a chapel – the only one of its kind in the world. The walk starts from a heath car park.

A free-running route for dogs through woods and fields in the company of other like-minded people, with the added benefit of a stream thrown in halfway round – who could ask for more?

Surrey – A Dog Walker's Guide

Terrain
A mainly flat walk on woodland paths and sandy bridleways.

Where to park
The Reigate Heath car park on Flanchford Road. **OS map:** Explorer 146 (GR TQ 239503).

How to get there
Flanchford Road is ¾ mile west of Reigate. Turn southwards off the A25 by a cricket ground and the car park is 500 metres on your left, with another parking area on your right.

Nearest refreshments
The **Skimmington Castle** is reached on a bridlepath from the car park, or by car by driving further down Flanchard Road and turning left along Bonnys Road. It welcomes dogs and serves a good selection of pub food.
☎ 01737 243100; www.skimmingtoncastle.co.uk

The Walk
. . . .

1 If you parked in the car park on the right-hand side of the road, take the path with the road behind you. If you parked on the left-hand side, cross the road and join the path. Follow this main path through the gorse and low heathland until you reach a wooden bench. Turn sharp left at the bench, which takes you along a path downhill through some trees. After 150 metres you will join a sandy track. Turn left.

2 Follow this track for 500 metres and at the bridleway sign, turn left. After the sign for **Heath Cottage**, bear right through the woods. This path will take you downhill with the golf course on your left-hand side. Follow this

Dog factors
. . . .
Distance: 2 miles.
Road walking: None, but you do come close to the busy A25 at point 5 where your dog should be under control.
Livestock: None.
Stiles: 1.
Nearest vets: Priory Vets, Reigate.

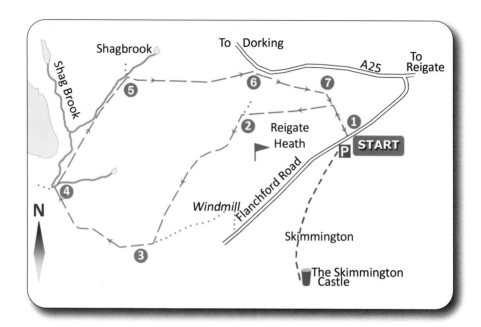

path as it bears left and walk through the woods and out onto the open heathland. You will be able to see **Reigate Heath windmill** on your left. Eventually you will reach some cottages on your right.

❸ Walk past the cottages and turn right, following the footpath sign into a field. Walk along the left-hand edge of the field, passing under a line of old oak trees, until you reach a gate. Go through the gate and follow the track downhill slightly into the woods.

❹ Just as you enter the woods there is a lovely stream that has spread into a ford and is perfect for dog swimming. In the summer the area is infused with the smell of the wild garlic that grows along the banks. Turn right in front of the stream and walk uphill and enter a field. Walk along the edge of the field, keeping the hedge to your left. As you reach a footpath sign, turn right, walking across the field to a large pine tree.

❺ At the pine tree turn left into the woods over a stile. Follow this footpath along the edge of a fenced field. At the end of the footpath you will reach a small road. Beware as you are now quite close to the A25. Cross over the road and bear right on the footpath through some trees until you reach a sandy lane.

6 Cross straight over this lane and walk uphill into the woods. At the top of the hill, bear left onto the footpath, which takes you through some pine trees.

7 On reaching the wooden bench, turn right and you are on the path straight back to the car park. *To walk to the **Skimmington Castle***, cross Flanchford Road and turn right onto the bridlepath to the pub.

A view of the windmill, seen from the golf course.

7

Langshott & the Burstow Stream

The footpath through the fields.

Sometimes, the best walks are ones that don't cross any formal parks or nature reserves, but are just hidden away from view in obscure areas. This is one of these, a circular walk from a friendly pub that follows the route of the Burstow Stream through woods and across fields and then loops back down a quiet lane and across some popular dog walking fields. The woods are simply jammed packed full of bluebells in spring and deer can be seen in the woods and fields.

As the route follows the stream, there is plenty of time for your dog to swim or wallow. The woods at the beginning of the walk are great for hunting and there are loads of hedges that hide all those elusive smells. The fields are regular dog walking haunts, so you can almost guarantee that you will meet another friendly owner.

Terrain

The walk itself is flat, but there are loads of stiles so it is a bit of a Grand National – but they are all easily accessed by dogs. If there has been heavy rain, the stream can flood.

Where to park

The Farmhouse pub at Langshott. Alternatively, if you are not planning any post-walk refreshments, parking is available approximately 100 metres further down Langshott on the right-hand side. **OS map:** Explorer 146 (GR TQ 288440).

How to get there

From the A23, turn off eastwards at the Chequers roundabout (with a large Shell petrol station in the centre of it). Drive under the railway bridge and the Farmhouse pub is 200 metres on the left.

Nearest refreshments

The **Farmhouse** is open for food all day and serves a good range of traditional pub grub, along with real ales and wines. Dogs are welcome in the bar and in the lovely, well-maintained garden. ☎ 01293 782146; www.thefarmhousehorley.co.uk

The Walk

. . . .

1 From the pub, turn left and walk all the way down this road, past **Langshott Manor Hotel** on your right and round a sharp right-hand bend.

2 After 400 metres, turn left just before **Keepers Cottage** down a public bridleway signposted to **Langshott Woods** and through a gate. You will have open woodland on your left and a fenced field on your right. Follow this path to the bridge over the stream. Cross the bridge and after 20 metres follow the path to the left, keeping the stream on your left as you cross an area of scrubland. In autumn this is a great blackberry-picking area. At the next bridge, cross over and head towards the electricity pylon and then left back towards the stream, crossing some more scrubland.

3 At the next bridge cross over and follow the path round to your left through some pine trees with a large fence on your right around a water treatment plant. At the end of this path, cross a stile into a field. Keeping the stream on

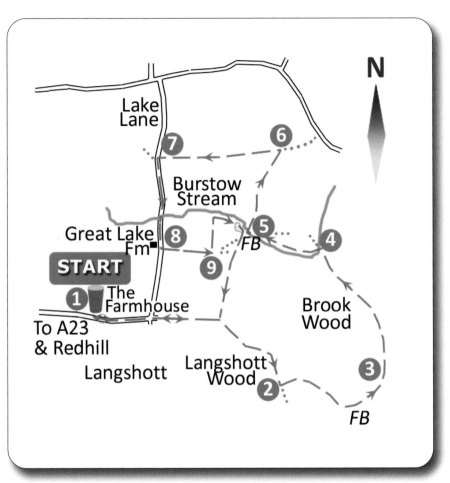

Dog factors

Distance: 3½ miles.
Road walking: A total of 850 metres on a very quiet country lane.
Livestock: There may be sheep in the fields.
Stiles: 13; all of which are dog-friendly.
Nearest vets: Gayton Veterinary Clinic, Horley.

Navigating one of the many bridges.

your left, follow this path along the side of the stream all the way across the fields over four sets of stiles between the hedges around the fields.

④ The fifth field boundary is a new wooden bridge with gates at either end. Cross this bridge and keep following the stream for another 400 metres until you reach another bridge over the stream.

⑤ *If you want to cut the walk short*, you can do so here by crossing the bridge and rejoining the route at point 9. *For the full walk*, bear right at the bridge and after 100 metres, cross another stile into a bluebell wood, and then go over another and out into a field. Cross straight over this field, then another stile in the hedge and walk towards the gate on the far side of the field.

⑥ Cross the stile at this gate and turn left, heading towards one of the old pill boxes that were placed here during the Second World War in case of invasion up the Burstow Stream. Go through the kissing gate at the pill box and cross the next three fields, until you come out via a kissing gate onto an unmade lane.

⑦ Turn left here and walk up the lane, re-crossing the stream and passing **Great Lake Farm** and **Puddle Duck Barn** on your right.

⑧ Just past the barn, turn left through a gate, following the footpath sign. At the field junction into the second field, turn left and follow the edge of the field round until you reach a pathway into the woods on your left, halfway along the bottom of the field. Take this pathway into the woods and turn right along the bank of the stream. Follow this path until you reach the other side of the bridge that you passed at point 5.

⑨ Walk past the bridge and straight up the footpath ahead of you until you pass through some woods, and rejoin **Langshott** just opposite the entrance to **Langshott Manor**. Turn right and walk back down to the **Farmhouse pub**.

8

Staffhurst & Great Earls woods

St Silvan's church.

This circular and gentle walk takes you through Staffhurst Wood, a fine mix of beech, oak and ash trees, to a pub and then back again through Great Earls Wood, past the very pretty St Silvan's church. Staffhurst Wood was used in the Second World War as an ammunition dump and this walk takes you along some of the brick paths that still remain. Great Earls Wood is

Dog factors

Distance: 2 miles.
Road walking: You need to cross four lanes, and there is 50 metres of road walking.
Livestock: There may be horses in the fields.
Stiles: 2, both with dog gates.
Nearest vets: Tanhouse Veterinary Clinic, Old Oxted.

full of sweet chestnut trees so in the autumn it is a perfect place to collect chestnuts. Both woods are carpeted with snowdrops and bluebells in the spring.

With the exception of a couple of fields that may contain horses, the walk through the woods can be without a lead. There are a couple of woodland ponds in Staffhurst Woods that make perfect dog dipping points on both the outward and return journeys. And you are bound to meet other dog walkers on the way round.

Terrain

A gentle walk through the trees, although the path in point 3 and across the fields, where the horses cut up the turf, can get muddy.

Where to park

The car park on Grants Lane. **OS map:** Explorer 147 (GR TQ 416484).

How to get there

Staffhurst Wood is 3 miles south of the A25 at Limpsfield. Take the B269 to the south and take the first right down Brick Kiln Lane. After 1 mile bear right onto Grants Lane. The car park is on your right after about 1½ miles.

Nearest refreshments

The **Royal Oak**, part of the Grumpy Mole group of pubs, halfway round the walk is a great place to stop. It has a good garden overlooking the fields, and dogs are allowed in the bar. A regularly changing menu of pub classics is on offer. ☎ 01883 722207; www.thegrumpymole.co.uk

The Walk

. . . .

1 From the car park, take the path past the metal barrier towards an information board. Just before you reach the information board, take the left-hand path signposted 'Tandridge Border Path'. This takes you down through the trees. After 200 metres, in front of the field, turn right onto a large footpath.

2 When you reach a metal gate to the corner of the field, take the left-hand footpath, following the edge of the field round. As you reach the end of the field, you will see a large woodland pond in front of you. Turn left in front of the pond, over a wooden boardwalk and head uphill. Keep straight on, ignoring any side paths. You will arrive at another set of boardwalks, cross over these and carry on uphill through the woods. You should still have the field on your left.

3 As you start walking away from the field, you reach a T-junction. Take the footpath to your right uphill. Follow this path through the woods as it winds to the right; beware as it can be muddy. Ignore a footpath sign to your left and then 50 metres on your right you will see a large deep pond in the woods; this is fed by a natural spring and it is said never to run dry. As the path exits into the open woodland again, turn left onto a wider path towards the road. You should have **Nutcracker Hall** and **Stone Cottage** in front of you.

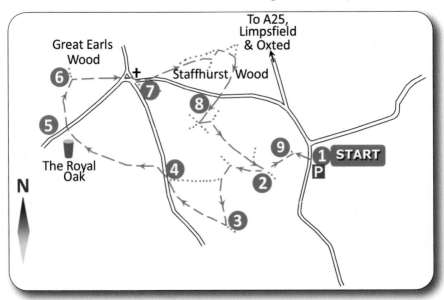

4 Cross the road and to the right take the footpath. At the end of the path through the trees there is a stile with a dog gate; this takes you into a field with horses, so dogs need to be under control. Cross this field with the fence on your left and pass through the gate into the next field. Cross this field to the right to the next stile, which has a wire panel that can be lifted for dog access. Follow the field with the hedge on your right as it winds to the left. At the gate, pass through it and turn immediately right up a small path. This takes you into the car park of the **Royal Oak**.

5 On leaving the Royal Oak, turn right out of the pub and cross the road, following the footpath sign into **Great & Little Earls Wood** through a kissing gate. Walk past the information sign and follow the path straight ahead of you into the sweet chestnut woods. After 200 metres, you will see a small wooden bench on your left, keep straight on.

6 Where the path forks, after 50 metres, take the right fork and you will pass through a thicket of holly. At the next footpath crossroads, on your right, there is a dedication plaque where a tree has been planted on the occasion of a silver wedding anniversary. Keep straight on. At the end of the path, you will see a wooden gate and another information board. Pass through the gate and cross the road in front of you and then the second road. On the corner to your left is **St Silvan's church**.

7 Keeping the church on your left walk down **Staffhurst Wood Road** for 50 metres and into St Silvan's car park on your left. Take the path at the far end of the car park, behind the information board marked with a Woodland Trust sign. This path takes you through some holly trees and downhill. As you pass some yew trees on your right, bear right, keeping on the path. As the path dips down into a sunken ditch, it bears left to reach a wooden gate. Pass through the gate onto a hard path and turn right. Follow this path to the gate and road at the end and cross straight over.

8 Follow this path through the woods downhill, ignoring any cross paths, until you reach a wide junction with a valley in front of you. Turn left here. This hard track is a legacy of the war, when rubble from the Blitz was recycled from London to provide the foundation for the tracks to the ammunition dumps. Follow this path downhill, with the valley on your right. At the bottom, you rejoin the footpath that you started on. Keep straight on with the field on your right and at the metal gate, keep straight on again, ignoring the path to your right that you used on the outward journey.

9 At the wooden horse barriers, turn right and you will be back at the car park.

Nutfield Marsh & Spynes Mere

Eyeing up the water birds on Spynes Mere.

Tucked between the A25, M23 and the M25, to the west of Redhill, there is a little nature oasis. Created from old sand and Fuller's Earth workings, the Nutfield Marsh Project consists of four wetland reserves: The Moors, Spynes Mere, Holmethorpe Lagoons and Mercers West, all situated along the Redhill Brook. Not only do they support a myriad of wetland wildlife, they are also very accessible via a network of well-maintained paths.

This walk takes you around the Spynes Mere Wetland Reserve, which consists of three lakes that at any time of year are teeming with birds and insects. The lakes themselves are well fenced, to protect both the wildlife and visitors. For dogs, the route is safe enough not to need any leads, and there are plenty of areas for chasing those pesky rabbits! As it is a popular dog walking area, you, and they, will nearly always be guaranteed some company along the way. Don't forget to take a pair of binoculars for your wildlife spotting.

Terrain

The majority of this walk is on well-maintained sandy or gravel paths, although in places the rabbits have caused some damage. The walk to and from the lake is across fields. The general terrain is gentle, with only one small slope around the back of the lake. Even in wet weather the ground is reasonably dry.

Where to park

Mercers Country Park, off Nutfield Marsh Road, Nutfield. **OS map:** Explorer 146 (GR TQ 300518).

How to get there

Turn off the A25 at Nutfield on Nutfield Marsh Road to reach the entrance to Mercers Park on the right. If approaching from Redhill, turn left down Cormongers Lane (just past a large office complex) and follow the lane downhill to a T-junction at the bottom. Turn right onto Nutfield Marsh Road, and the entrance to Mercers Park is about ½ mile on your left.

Nearest refreshments

The **Inn on the Pond** on Nutfield Marsh Road offers home-cooked food and a range of good beers and wine. Dogs are allowed in the garden and in the bar area if they are well behaved. You can take a detour on the walk to the inn (see point 5) and then walk back to the car park if you wish. ☎ 01737 643000; www.theinnonthepondnutfield.co.uk

Dog factors

· ·

Distance: 2 miles.
Road walking: None if you do just the lake walk. Approximately 250 metres of country lane if you detour to the pub.
Livestock: Tethered horses on the marsh.
Stiles: 2; suitable for dogs of any size.
Nearest vets: Village Veterinary Centre, Merstham.

The Walk

. . . .

1 From the car park in **Mercers Park**, walk towards the **Aquasports Centre** at the eastern end of **Mercers Lake**. Keeping the centre on your left, walk between the clubhouse and the boat storage area through a small gate into a grassed field. Cross this field, making your way to the stile in the hedge on the far side by a large oak tree.

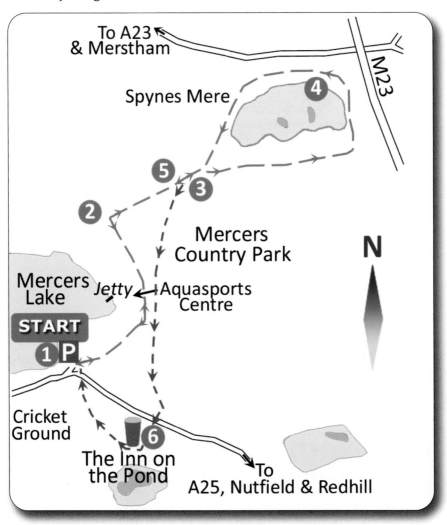

The water reserve at point 4 of the walk.

2 Pass through a gate onto a sandy footpath between well-maintained hedges. Follow the sandy footpath with hedges on both sides until another footpath joins from the right. At this stage you bear left and then right again. On your left is the smaller of the lakes, and if your dogs like a swim, they might find the gap in the hedge and the access to the stream that runs beneath the path.

3 After about 200 metres you will come to a junction where the footpath either branches to the left or carries straight on through a gate. Pass through the gate and you will be able to see the main lake to your left. Don't worry if the hedge blocks your view as you will come to a better vantage point further on. On your right-hand side, watch out for the flocks of Canada geese on the farmland behind the restored wetland. Continue bearing left along this pathway as it follows the rim of the lake.

4 As you pass the eastern end of the lake, the path begins to climb gently until you come out on a grassy vantage point from where you have a fantastic view and a great excuse to catch your breath. Still keeping the lake on your left, continue along the path for about 500 metres until you reach a gate that leads you onto a wider path (which is actually part of the National Cycleway – so watch out for cyclists). Ahead of you is **Mercers West**, one of the other restored quarries. With **Spynes Mere** on your left, follow the path downhill between the two lakes until it rejoins the footpath that you followed from the car park. Turn right and you retrace your steps to the car park over the two stiles and back past the **Aquasports clubhouse**. You can stop and enjoy the sight of the small sailing boats and windsurfers on a good day.

5 *If you want to make a detour to the **Inn on the Pond***, after the left and right dogleg, rather than carrying straight on to the Aquasports Centre, take the left-hand footpath. This leads you across some open fields. Take care as there are often horses or sheep in the right-hand fields, although they are usually fenced in securely. At the end of the fields you pass through a gate and onto a narrow lane. This takes you past some restored barns on your right and some cottages and houses. Continue straight down this lane. Beware of the horses tethered on the marshland to your right as you pass the last house. At the main road cross straight over, keeping the pond on your right, and the inn is around the corner after about 50 metres.

6 To return to the car park from the inn, leave at the front and turn left down the footpath adjacent to the cricket ground. Follow this path to the cricket pavilion and then bear right across the marsh towards the road. Again beware of the horses tethered on the marsh. On reaching the road, cross over and walk approximately 50 metres along to the left to reach the car park entrance.

10

Mickleham & Box Hill

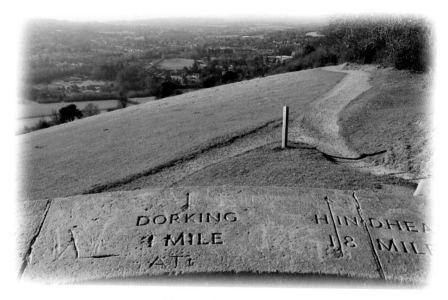

The view from Box Hill.

This is a strenuous walk starting and finishing in the village of Mickleham but the effort is worth it as the route takes in Box Hill, a prominent Surrey landmark and probably the best known part of the North Downs. Box Hill derives its name from the rare box trees that grow on its lower slopes and on a clear day you can see for 25 miles south from the Salomons Memorial Viewpoint at the top, where there is a café and visitor centre. You will also cross the River Mole by the stepping stones on the site of the original ford used on the Pilgrims' Way, before making your way back through the open parkland of Norbury Park.

Dogs can enjoy off-lead walking across the whole of Box Hill and as you go up through the woods you will see some of the best yew woodlands in southern England before reaching the mixed deciduous trees at the top. Halfway round they can have a lovely swim in the river at the stepping stones (although there is a bridge for non-swimming dogs). Norbury Park at the end of the walk is a Site of Special Scientific Interest and its managed grassland is great for dogs to run free.

Terrain
The walk starts with quite a challenging climb before descending into a valley via some steps and then there is a steady climb up Juniper Bottom. The way down is a series of steps, which can be slippery, through the woods. If your dog can't or won't swim, take the footpath to the bridge over the River Mole, as opposed to the stepping stones. The walk crosses the busy A24 twice, once via an underpass and the other time by a footpath over the main road, but it is worth it.

Where to park
Behind the Running Horses pub in Mickleham on a quiet lane. **OS map:** Explorer 146 (GR TQ 169534).

How to get there
From the A24 north of Dorking, take the B2209 past the Mercure Box Hill, Burford Bridge Hotel. Follow this road up to Mickleham and turn left just past the Running Horses pub to park.

Nearest refreshments
The **Running Horses** in Mickleham is a walker- and dog-friendly pub. A range of upmarket pub dishes is available in the bar, along with real ales and a comprehensive wine list. Booking is recommended. ☎ 01372 372279; www.therunninghorses.co.uk

At the top of Box Hill you will find a **National Trust shop**, visitor centre and a servery that sells freshly-made sandwiches, soups, cakes and biscuits.

Dog factors
Distance: 5½ miles.
Road walking: 50 metres through Mickleham to the footpath; 500 metres along Crabtree Lane to Westhumble station and another 400 metres of farm lane on exiting Norbury Park.
Livestock: There may be sheep in fields on your right at point 1 and on Juniper Bottom at point 3. Watch your dogs on the electric fence that encloses the sheep.
Stiles: 1.
Nearest vets: Denbies View Veterinary Centre, Dorking.

Halfway round the walk, you will find the **Stepping Stones** pub at Westhumble, which serves more traditional snacks, jacket potatoes, sandwiches and bar meals. Dogs are welcome in the bar. ☎ 01306 889932; www.steppingstonesdorking.com

The Walk

. . . .

1 From the **Running Horses pub**, turn right and walk along the road past **St Peter's church**. Take the left turn up a driveway past the church, alongside the graveyard, following the footpath sign. Just before the private sign, cross the stile on the right, which takes you up through the woods. There can be sheep in the field to your right but it is well fenced. As the path starts to veer away from the field, take the right path at the footpath marker up quite a steep hill to a wide footpath (**Thames Down Link**) and an information board for the Box Hill estate – keep straight ahead uphill.

2 At the next footpath marker turn right and then left into some conifers and at the fence post right again and you will come out onto a viewpoint with a bench. Keep straight ahead with the bench behind you and follow the path down some steps.

3 Cross straight over the road at the bottom of the steps, go through the car park and take the public bridleway, ignoring the footpath sign on your left. Follow this path up **Box Hill**.

4 At the top of the hill, as you enter the yew woods, take the first pathway on your right, following the nature walk sign. At the next junction, take the second right turn through some deciduous woodland. Turn left at the next T-junction onto a wide path, which will bring you out onto **Donkey Green**. Keeping the green on your left, follow the path round to the car park and the visitor centre is straight ahead of you.

5 Leaving the visitor centre, turn right and take the footpath past the Swiss cottage where John Logie Baird carried out some of his first experiments in television and carry on to the **Salomons Memorial Viewpoint** – so called as it was Leopold Salomons who bought Box Hill for the National Trust in 1913.

6 Take the footpath underneath the viewpoint to your right into some trees and then turn left, following the signs for the **North Downs Way** down steps to the bottom. Ignore the sign to the Stepping Stones footbridge on your right and cross the stepping stones. If your dog won't swim, take the path to the bridge and rejoin at point 8.

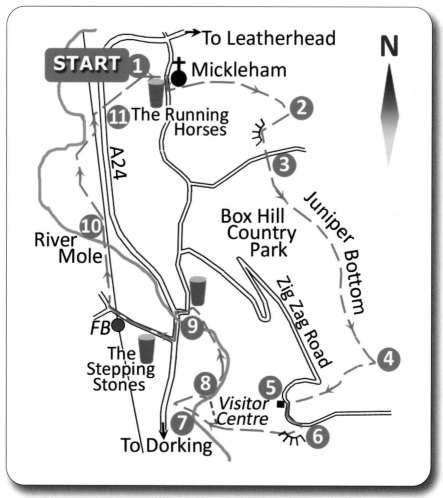

7 From the stepping stones, walk up to the car park and take the right-hand footpath, which takes you down to the river again.

8 Walk past the bridge and follow the river all the way along through the meadows until you see the A24 in front of you.

9 Turn left and cross under the road via the underpass. Turn left out of the underpass and right up **Westhumble Street**. The **Stepping Stones pub** is on your left-hand side. Follow this road for 500 metres to **Westhumble railway**

station, cross the bridge and take the footpath immediately to your right down through a kissing gate into **Norbury Park**, a Surrey Wildlife Park Site of Special Scientific Interest. Follow the footpath along the side of the railway line, crossing another bridge over the river. You will be able to see **Norbury Park House** ahead of you to the left.

10 After 50 metres, go through a gate, ignoring the underpass to your right. After another 50 metres the path veers to the left across the field. At the end of the field go through a kissing gate and turn right onto a quiet lane. Follow this lane, passing underneath the railway line.

11 After 50 metres, take a small footpath up a bank to your right and cross the A24 through a kissing gate on the other side. Follow the footpath through the hedge, then another kissing gate and across a field on the diagonal. Exit the field and walk straight up the lane in front of you to arrive at the rear of the **Running Horses**.

Crossing the stepping stones.

Margery Wood & Banstead Heath

Looking back at point 7 of the route.

Atremendous walk, with the majority being across some of the 760 acres of Banstead Heath. This is one of the four areas that make up the Banstead Commons, which are owned by the local council and managed by specially-appointed conservators, with the purpose of maintaining the commons for the benefit of the public. Nearly all the heath is open meadow but the walk takes a circular route from Margery Wood, a small National Trust woodland that has a marvellous display of bluebells in the spring and encompasses the mixed oak and birch woods of the heath. An added benefit is the Sportsman pub at Mogador – a very dog-friendly establishment, which is near the end of the route.

Give dogs some common land and they will be happy. This walk is criss-crossed with paths used every day by dog walkers, so they are bound to make some new friends and will have a great time sniffing out all the ones that they miss!

Terrain

This is an easy walk with no steep hills. Across the common, the paths are grass although the route to and from Margery Wood, on a bridleway, can be a bit muddy in wet weather.

Where to park

The Margery Wood National Trust car park. **OS map:** Explorer 146 (GR TQ 245527).

How to get there

From junction 8 of the M25 go north on the A217. Take the first left all the way to the end and Margery Wood car park is on your left.

Nearest refreshments

The **Sportsman** at Mogador is well known as a dog-friendly pub and serves a wide range of pub food all day long. It has a huge garden. ☎ 01737 246655; www.sportsman.timewellspent.co.uk

The Walk

- -

❶ Facing the entrance to the car park, take the bridleway to the right, so that you are walking alongside with the car park on your left. Follow this public bridleway as it winds its way along the edge of the woods. You will have fields on your right and a great view across Surrey to the north. At the end of the woods the path runs between two fields that may contain horses and then down into a dip and up again back into some woods.

Dog factors

- -

Distance: 4 miles.
Road walking: About 50 metres on quiet lanes on the way to the heath and 100 metres of quiet lane on leaving the Sportsman.
Livestock: None.
Stiles: None.
Nearest vets: Banstead Village Vets, Banstead.

2 As you reach a narrow tarmac road, cross straight over, keeping the house on your right-hand side. After another 100 metres, just before you reach a second road, turn right down a path that runs adjacent to it. At the end of this path, at the road, turn right and cross over past **Walton Gorse**, and take the bridlepath signposted to the left. Some 20 metres further on, cross straight over the driveways to the houses and follow the blue bridleway signs into the woods. Follow this path through the woods and, after 500 metres, bear left at the junction.

3 When you see an information board in front of you, turn right onto the footpath that follows the edge of the woodland. You will have **Walton Heath Golf Course** on your left-hand side and woods on your right. As you reach the end of the woods you come out onto **Banstead Heath**. Turn left and follow the footpath all the way along the edge of the heath towards the woods in the distance. The golf course is on your left and open grassland on your right. Some 50 metres before you reach the woods, there is a pond suitable for your dog to have a dip on your left-hand side.

4 As you reach the woods, turn right along the edge, with the remains of a hedge on your right-hand side.

5 At the first permissive ride sign, take the left-hand path into the woods, keeping straight ahead past a solitary silver birch tree in a clearing. This wide-sweeping path follows a wide arc through the woods. Stay on this path, ignoring any side paths or bridleways, until you reach a waymarker.

6 Turn right 20 metres after that, just before some wooden gateposts and a silver birch wood fence. Keep on this path until you come out onto the open heathland again. Continue straight ahead, following the permissive ride sign and the path goes downhill, with

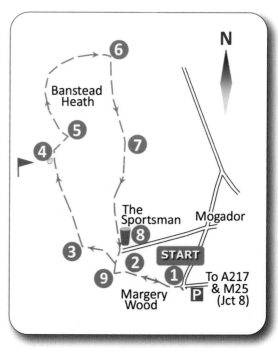

woodland on your left. At the bottom of the hill, bear left through the woods and then after 50 metres exit the woods and turn right, following the footpath all the way along the edge of the woods on your right. The path heads up a gentle hill and you will be able to see another information board ahead of you.

7 Some 20 metres before the board, bear right and you should now have grassland on your right and woods on your left. At the end of the heathland, at the third information board, bear left off the common and you will see the **Sportsman pub** on your left.

8 On leaving the Sportsman, turn left down the road. At the junction at the end, turn right past the 'No Unauthorised Vehicle Sign' and then left along the road.

9 Just before the big white house, take the left-hand footpath that runs parallel to the lane and after 75 metres, turn left back onto the bridleway; this leads back to the car park.

Banstead Heath.

Epsom Downs

On the downs.

Epsom Downs is, of course, famous for being the home of the Derby. The racecourse, with its buildings and car parks, dominates the north side. This walk takes you across the downs and the racetrack, and along bridleways to the village of Walton on the Hill, and then back through woods. The views on your way across the downs are quite spectacular so do make sure to go on a clear day. You can break the walk at Walton on the Hill and enjoy a drink at the Bell or, alternatively, stop at the Rubbing House on your return.

As you cross the downs the dogs can run free, while you take in the sounds of the skylarks and other birds that are indigenous to the area and, as it is a popular walking location, they can enjoy the company of other dogs.

Dog factors

Distance: 4½ miles.
Road walking: 100 metres of restricted access lanes.
Livestock: Horses train on the downs between 6.15 am and 12 noon, so do beware and keep your dog under control. There are horses in the fields along the route, but you only walk through one field, the rest are fenced.
Stiles: None.
Nearest vets: Winton Lodge Vets, Epsom.

There are also plenty of woods for hunting and many new smells on the bridlepaths.

NB: Do check beforehand that there is not racing on the day you intend to visit (www.epsomdowns.co.uk).

Terrain

By the nature of the landscape, this is an up-and-down hill walk although the hills are mostly gentle, with long inclines. Most of the downs are grassland and the bridlepaths are all well maintained and mostly laid to stone chips.

Where to park

Outside the Rubbing House pub on Epsom Downs – but do not park in their car park as you may get clamped. **OS map:** Explorer 146 (GR TQ 215585).

How to get there

Turn off the A217 between Tadworth and Banstead, onto the A240. Turn left at the traffic lights after the large Asda store. At the T-junction, turn right and follow the road round the racecourse. Go straight over the first roundabout and then take the first left at the second, past the main grandstand. At the traffic lights, turn left and drive under the racecourse, turning immediately left after the bridge. Park at the top of the hill in front of the pub.

Nearest refreshments

The **Bell**, aka the Rat, at Walton on the Hill welcomes dogs as long as they are on a lead. Serves drinks only at lunchtimes. ☎ 01737 812132; www.thebell-therat.co.uk

The **Rubbing House** at Epsom Racecourse has a large garden overlooking the course and dogs are allowed in the garden. There is a wide selection of food and sandwiches. ☎ 01372 745050; www.rubbinghouse.com

Surrey – A Dog Walker's Guide

The Walk

1 From where you have parked, with the grandstand and the **Rubbing House pub** behind you, follow the footpath sign across the racecourse. This takes you downhill across some of the training gallops and then back uphill to the main racetrack with its white fence posts. Cross the access road before the track and then cross the track at the footpath point. Take a moment to look back and enjoy the view of the course.

2 After crossing the racetrack turn left and then right, following the footpath through the scrub. After 50 metres the scrub opens up. Keep following the footpath alongside the hedge. As the scrub gives way to grassland, beware as you have to cross the training track and horses have priority between 6.15 am and 12 noon daily. Cross straight over the track and the grassland beyond, heading towards a second fenced training track. Cross the second track into some woods. You will have woods on your left and the rear of houses and gardens on your right.

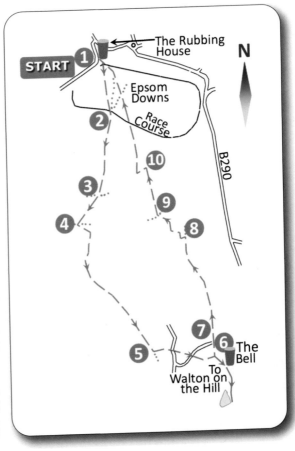

3 Follow this path until you exit the woods onto some more gallops. Bear slightly right cross the gallops with the woods behind you whilst walking downhill.

4 At the bottom of the hill, cross another training track with white railing, then cross over a small bridleway and turn left, following the public bridleway sign to Walton on the Hill. After 50 metres, at **Nohome Farm**, turn right up the public bridleway. Follow this path all the way up the hill, enjoying the views to your right across the downs with **Downs View Wood** beneath you.

5 Just before you reach the houses on your left, climb over the stile into a field on your left. Cross the field, keeping the hedge on your right, then climb another stile and bear right up a quiet lane. After 25 metres, turn left over a stile, down a very narrow footpath that leads between the gardens and fields. At the end of this path, climb over the stile onto a restricted byway, and head straight across over another stile onto another footpath between houses and fields. At the end of this footpath, cross another stile and turn left. You should have a fence on your left and a hedge on your right.

6 Bear right at the end of the path through a big white iron gate, up a wide un-made-up track to the **Bell pub**. If you want to continue into **Walton on the Hill** – follow this path for about 500 metres to the village pond. To return, retrace your steps to the big white iron gate and turn right, passing the footpath that you walked up. At the bottom of the hill, turn right onto the restricted byway, and after 50 metres, turn left down the public bridleway, adjacent to **Bridle Cottage**.

7 Follow this footpath all the way downhill, past the back of gardens. The fields to your left are popular dog walking areas and open for access.

8 At the bottom of the hill, as you reach the end of the houses and enter the woods, turn left towards the information board. Turn right at the board and then after 50 metres, turn left. Follow this path all the way through the trees, crossing another path.

9 At the edge of the woods, cross a sandy gallop, and head uphill onto the downs by the '3 furlong' sign towards the woods.

10 On reaching the woods, turn left and follow the trees around and then right onto a bridleway. Follow this bridleway across an open area and bear left into another section of woods. On exiting the woods, you will see the white rails of the main racecourse ahead. You will be on a bridleway so follow it up towards them, cross the racecourse again, and keep following the footpath back across the downs to where you have parked your car.

West End & Esher Common

The pond at West End.

West End, to the west of Esher, is a small village that is centred around a pretty village green with a pond. It's also where you can find Garsons, a garden centre, farm shop and 'pick your own' farm that has been in the same family since 1871. This walk from the village green takes in some of Esher Common, with its myriad of hidden ponds, boardwalks alongside the River Mole and Winterdown Wood, a popular dog walking area criss-crossed with tracks and paths.

A splendid route for dogs, as they can wallow in the ponds and spend time hunting out new friends and all sorts of wildlife in the woods.

Dog factors

Distance: 3½ miles.
Road walking: None.
Livestock: None.
Stiles: None.
Nearest vets: Medivet Esher.

Terrain

Through the common the paths are well managed. The path along the edge of the River Mole crosses some boardwalks that can be very slippery in the wet. In areas the path can get muddy. The path down to the river is via some steps and then the route back up is quite a steep climb.

Where to park

On West End village green adjacent to the pond. **OS map:** Explorer 161 (GR TQ 128639).

How to get there

Turn off the A307 on West End Lane, opposite the entrance to Claremont Gardens, 1 mile south of Esher. This will bring you down onto West End Green. Park near the pond.

Nearest refreshments

The **Prince of Wales** pub is on the corner of the green at West End. Part of a chain, they serve traditional pub fayre, morning coffee and afternoon tea. Dogs are allowed in the garden. ☎ 01372 465483; www.chefandbrewer.com

The Walk

❶ With the pond behind you, walk towards the woods at the end of the green. Pass a wooden bench on your right and enter the woods. You will see Halfpenny Pond on your left and then you pass through some wooden barriers and over a little bridge. Take the path heading away from the pond. This is a dead straight path through the woods.

❷ After 200 metres, turn right into the woods, leaving the straight path. Keep to

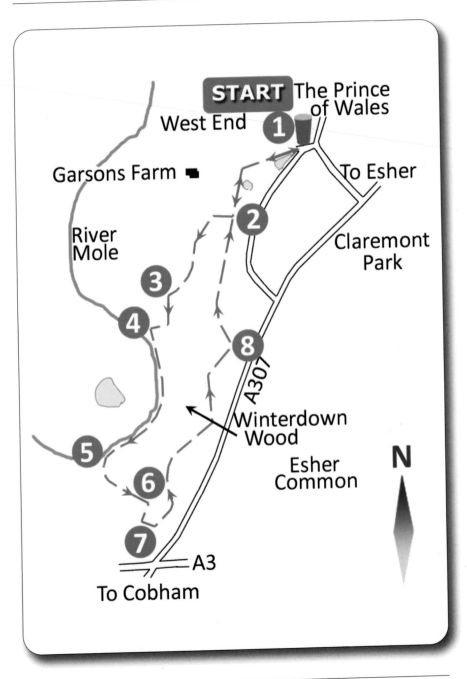

this path, and as you exit the woods, you will see **Margy Pond** on your left-hand side. Follow the path all the way round the pond, over a small wooden bridge and back into the woods. Continue on this path as it twists and turns through the woods – it is clear as it is well worn. Watch out for tree roots under the leaves After 800 metres, exit the woods into an area of cleared woodland and walk past a large wooden bench on your right and **Lardy Pond**. As you reach the second bench at the end of the pond, follow the path around to your left.

3 As you exit the woods, you will see a hedge in front of you. Turn left onto a main footpath alongside this fence on the edge of the 'pick your own' fields of **Garsons Farm**. At the end of the field as you reach the woods, turn right and head uphill, keeping the field on your right-hand side.

4 At the top of the hill, there is a bench where you can stop to catch your breath and enjoy the fantastic views of the river valley and farmland below you. To the left of the bench there is an access path to the river walk and boardwalk. Take this path down some steps to the bottom where you reach the river and

Benson by the River Mole.

turn left along the bank, following the footpath over the boardwalks that cross the steeper and muddier areas of the bank. At the end of the boardwalks, keep following the river bank and as you reach a bench, ignore the sign to the car park up the steps to your left. Keep straight on, following the river bank until you can go no further and there is a fence in front of you.

5 Turn left, walking uphill with a stream on your right-hand side. This is quite a steep hill. As you enter the taller beech trees, keep heading uphill towards the rhododendrons; do not follow the line of beech trees along the valley. At the rhododendrons bear left through the bushes and you will reach a fence with a gate in it.

6 Turn right here and follow the fence downhill to a small valley with a bridge over the stream – a perfect dog swimming pool. Cross the bridge and follow the path up the hill with the fence still on your left-hand side.

7 As you reach the top of the hill, you will see a wooden fence in front of you; turn left down an avenue of conifer trees, past an entrance to a house on your left. At the end of the trees, turn left onto a footpath back into the woods. Cross straight over a small access road and over a small bridge. As you reach a crossing in some silver birch trees, go straight over. You will see a large house on your right amongst the trees and then you will pass under the electricity lines. Keep straight on into beech and birch woods. At an old gnarled oak tree, 100 metres into the woods, turn left onto a slightly sunken footpath, ignoring the path straight ahead, which has two wooden marker posts in front of it. At the first junction, turn left downhill and at the bottom of the hill, turn right in front of a wooden bench. Follow this footpath through the trees over a sandy bank, keeping towards the left.

8 As you exit onto the open ground, take the left fork and follow the path down through the open scrubland and you will see another large bench and some wooden barriers in front of you – pass through these and you will see another pond. Walk round the pond to the left and you arrive back at the very end of the straight path that you started the walk on. Follow the path back to the green and your car.

14

Sheepleas

Benson at the Millennium Viewpoint.

Sheepleas lies just south of the village of West Horsley and has been designated a Site of Special Scientific Interest. It is a mosaic of woodlands and grassland and, as such, is home to a multitude of wild flowers and butterflies. If you are looking for a gentle walk through some lovely woodland that reflects the changing seasons and all that is great about nature, you need look no further. St Mary's church at the halfway point has a very pretty churchyard, which in the spring is simply carpeted with snowdrops. This walk has the added benefit of being stile free and is therefore suitable for the less mobile and indeed, for those walking with buggies.

A completely safe walk for dogs, with squirrels, rabbits and deer to keep them happy, along with the scents and smells of all the other dogs that use these popular woods.

Terrain

The walk undulates up and down some gentle slopes on woodland paths and bridleways.

Where to park

In the Shere Road car park for Sheepleas. **OS map:** Explorer 145 (GR TQ 085513).

How to get there

Turn southwards off the A246 at the West Horsley roundabout, down Shere Road. The car park is situated about ½ mile on your left.

Nearest refreshments

The very dog-friendly **King William IV** at West Horsley is a short drive away in the centre of the village. A good range of freshly-cooked pub food is available. ☎ 01483 282318; www.kingwilliam4th.com

The Walk

1 From the car park, take the path adjacent to the information board that heads away downhill. This path leads down through the woods into a valley. At the bottom of the hill, cross over the main path and bear left uphill following the signs to **St Mary's car park**.

2 After 50 metres you will reach a picnic area on your right-hand side. Keep straight on and at the end of the area you will reach the **Millennium Viewpoint** where, on a good day, you can see the London Eye. There is a bench where you can pause to enjoy the view. With the viewpoint on your right, follow the path downhill again through some open grassland until you reach the valley at the bottom.

Dog factors

Distance: 2 miles.
Road walking: None.
Livestock: None.
Stiles: None.
Nearest vets: Brelades Vets, Bookham.

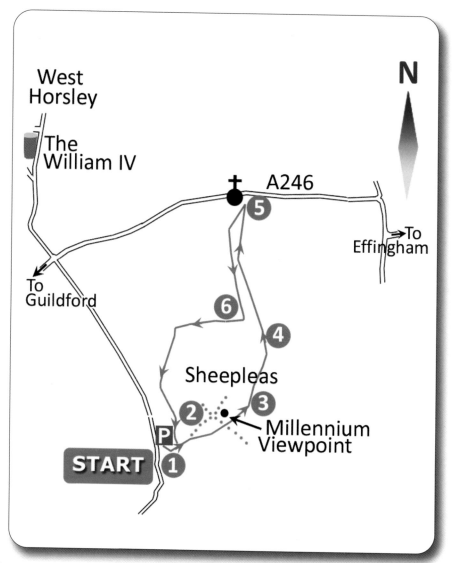

West
Horsley

The
William IV

A246

N

† 5

To
Effingham

To
Guildford

6

4

Sheepleas

2 3

P Millennium
Viewpoint

START 1

3 Bear left along the bottom of the valley and after 100 metres you will enter some woods. Follow the footpath through these woods, crossing over a wide track, and you will exit onto one of the grassland areas of the site. Walk along the footpath crossing the grassland until you reach the woods on the other side. Take the path through the woods and exit onto a second grassland area.

4 Follow the footpath along the left-hand side of the grassland. At the end of the field, exit through a push gate and take the right-hand path alongside the woodland on your left and a fenced field on your right.

5 After about 200 metres you will see **St Mary's church** on your left. Stop to enjoy the pretty graveyard. To return, with the church behind you, cross the car park behind the church and enter the woods to the right of the information board. This path takes you back into the woods. After 150 metres, you reach a crossroads; keep straight on and again where the path joins a bridleway.

6 As you walk down into a clearing, turn right uphill, so that you have a field on your right and the woods on your left. Keep following this footpath as it takes you through some magnificent avenues of trees. As you reach some broken wooden fences on your right, keep straight on until you rejoin the footpath that leads down from the car park. Turn right and walk back uphill to your car.

St Mary's churchyard in springtime.

St Martha's Hill & Chilworth

The millstones seen along the way.

This walk starts off at the top of St Martha's Hill where St Martha's church is perched on its summit, on the old Pilgrims' Way, with its simply stunning views across the county. From there it winds down a steep hill to the valley bottom past Chilworth Manor and you follow the meandering route of the Tilling Bourne through Chilworth's old gunpowder mills, where you can take a diversion to the Percy Arms, before making your way back, over fields and past Albury Mill and through some ancient woodland.

If your dog loves swimming, this is the ideal walk – the streams in the valley are clear, shallow and safe and, on a hot day, the old gunpowder mills are

Dog factors

Distance: 3½ miles.
Road walking: 200 metres down Halfpenny Lane to the gunpowder mills and another 200 metres through Albury Mill on a private road.
Livestock: There can be horses in the fields and watch out for wildfowl on the mill ponds.
Stiles: 4.
Nearest vets: Brelades Vets, Gomshall.

shaded by a deciduous green canopy of trees. The start and finish of the walk take you through open woodland where dogs can run and hunt to their heart's content.

Terrain
There is quite a steep climb up to the church at the start of the walk and then a very steep path downhill so it might be worthwhile taking a walking stick. Along the valley bottom the path is well maintained. The route back up to the car park is slightly less strenuous.

Where to park
St Martha's church car park. **OS map:** Explorer 145 (GR TQ 035485).

How to get there
From the A25 between Guildford and Dorking, take the A248 through Albury. As you leave Albury, take the second right up Guildford Lane, immediately after a sharp left-hand bend. After about a mile turn left into St Martha's church car park.

Nearest refreshments
The **Percy Arm**s in Chilworth is a good pub serving a wide range of pub food and grills. Dogs are allowed in the bar area and in the garden. ☎ 01483 561765; www.thepercyarms.net

The **Drummond Arms** in Albury is a short drive back along the A248 on the left-hand side. It welcomes dogs in the garden and serves a good range of delicious home-cooked food, along with real ales and a good selection of wines. The pub has a lovely setting at the side of the stream. ☎ 01483 202039; www.thedrummondarms.co.uk

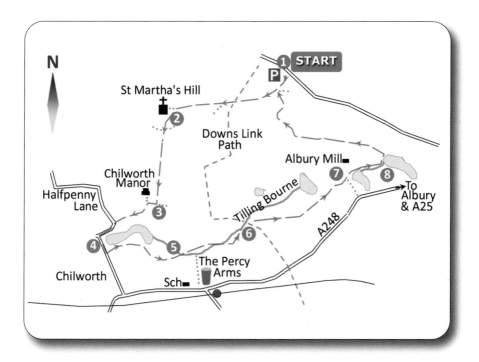

The Walk

. . . .

1 From the car park, with your back to the road, follow the public footpath signs adjacent to the information board. After 50 metres you join a bridleway – turn right onto this wide sandy path through the woods. Keep on the bridleway, ignoring a 'Downs Link Way' sign to the left, and then after 20 metres follow the fingerpost to the left. At the next fingerpost keep right and this path will lead you up quite a steep hill to **St Martha's church**. Take a few minutes to catch your breath and enjoy the views from one of the many benches that are strategically placed around the church.

2 Take the footpath to the left of the church as you face it, along below the church and as you pass it, turn left so that it is behind you as you head downhill. After 100 metres cross straight over the footpath junction onto a steep footpath through the woods. Do beware as this path is VERY steep in places. As you leave the woods, ignore the footpath sign on your left and keep straight on. You should have a house on your right; watch out for the llamas in the field on your right although they are well fenced in.

Cooling off in one of the millstreams.

3 At the public bridleway, turn right onto the driveway of **Chilworth Manor** and then left downhill. At the end of the bridleway turn left onto **Halfpenny Lane**. Follow the lane down and round a sharp left turn over two bridges.

4 After the second bridge, turn left into the green gates of **Chilworth Gunpowder Mills**. With the gates behind you, follow the footpath through the mills and the woods. You will have some trout fishing ponds on your left and eventually you will pass the remains of the mill grinding stones on your left.

5 After 400 metres there is a path to your right over a small footbridge. *If you want to visit the* **Percy Arms**, *follow the path up between the fields and after about 500 metres you will pass a school on your left. At the road, turn left and the pub is 200 metres on your left. To rejoin the walk, retrace your steps to the footbridge and turn right. To continue the walk,* keep following this path past some picnic tables, ignoring a left-hand branch and walk past the ruins of the old mill buildings on your left.

6 At the end of the path turn right onto a bridleway, go over a bridge and cross the stile on your left into a field. Cross this field to another stile and then, keeping the ditch on your right, cross the second field to a telegraph pole. Cross a third stile, go over a small ditch and follow the footpath through the field. As you reach brambles on your right, turn right over a fourth stile and onto a narrow path between the field and a garden.

7 At the lane, ignore the sharp left turn, but walk to the left past **Albury Mills**, with **Mill Reach** and the large **Postford Pond** on your right. Follow this lane all the way to the end as it winds alongside the mill pond. Bear left at the end, ignoring the footpath sign on your right.

8 At the pale green house on your left, take the footpath to the left over some boardwalks; this leads up past the back of the house, which should now be on your left. Follow this path through the woods with the river down in the valley on your left. After some holly bushes, turn right back uphill, following the path. When you reach a field on your left, turn right so that the field is behind you – there is no footpath sign. After 200 metres, bear left, following the footpath sign, and then at the top of the hill head straight ahead, following the South Downs Trail marker. In 50 metres you rejoin the car park.

Ripley & the Wey Navigation

The Wey Navigation.

This is a winding, circular walk that takes you through a range of different sights and scenery, with something new at every turn. You start off in the very pretty Ripley village, with its good range of shops and restaurants, and walk up through woods, past the historic Ockham Mill over the River Wey and join the Wey Navigation, with its colourful canal boats, to Pyrford Lock where you can stop at the Anchor pub. On the return journey you cross Pyrford golf course and circumnavigate Pyrford Green village across arable fields, before re-crossing the navigation at Walsham Lock and making your way back to Ripley.

A lovely walk for dogs, as they can run free for most of the way and enjoy hunting in the woods, swimming in the river and ditches, rabbiting in the fields and making friends with other dogs on the way. The lanes that you cross or walk along are all quiet so easy to follow with dogs.

Terrain

Very easy going; most of the footpaths are well maintained although the paths across the fields and through the woods could get muddy in wet weather.

Where to park

Ripley village green car park, at the end close to the cricket club. **OS map:** Explorer 145 (GR TQ 055569).

How to get there

From the A3, take the B2215 to Ripley. Turn right in Ripley High Street where parking is signposted and then right again to park close to the cricket club in the farthest car park.

Nearest refreshments

The **Anchor** pub at Pyrford Lock has a large garden from where you can watch the boats waiting to pass through the lock. Dogs are allowed in one area of the pub and in the garden. A traditional selection of pub food, real ales and wines is available. ☎ 01932 342507; www.anchorpyrford.co.uk

The **Seven Stars** on Newark Lane, about a mile from the centre of Ripley, serves a good range of food and real ales and although dogs aren't allowed in the pub itself, there are wooden heated dining booths in the garden – perfect for lunch with a wet canine! ☎ 01483 225128; www.sevenstarsripley.co.uk

For something a little more sophisticated, the **Talbot** in Ripley High Street has an AA Rosette for its food. Dogs are allowed in the bar and the garden. ☎ 01483 225188; www.bespokehotels.com

Dog factors
. . . .

Distance: 4 miles.
Road walking: 100 metres across Pyrford Lock and then you need to cross the road in Pyrford village. There is then another 200 metres along Warren Lane. The lane down to Walsham Lock is a private road with limited traffic.
Livestock: There may be horses in the fields, but they are all well fenced.
Stiles: 1.
Nearest vets: Cobham Veterinary Centre, Cobham.

The Walk

• •

1 From the car park, with your back to the **High Street**, walk round the edge of the cricket pitch to your right, so that you pass the clubhouse on your right. Head towards a large, spreading oak tree and walk between that and the cricket nets, towards the woods. As you enter the woods, turn left onto the footpath at the waymarker. Follow this path as it meanders through the woods. There are some very pretty miniature oaks lining the pathway.

2 After you pass a fingerpost, the path splits. Take the right-hand fork and after 100 metres you will cross a wooden bridge over a ditch onto a wide bridlepath between some fields that could have horses in them. Cross a second wooden bridge and you will come out onto **Mill Lane**.

3 Turn left onto Mill Lane and walk down through a wooden gate that says 'Private road & weak bridge'. This takes you through **Ockham Mill**. You walk down between the mill and the weir and over the bridge. Then turn right alongside the mill tail, following the private road. At the end of the lane, pass back through a gate onto another bridleway. Follow this path over some scrub land and another couple of wooden bridges. You will see **Wisley golf course** on your right-hand side.

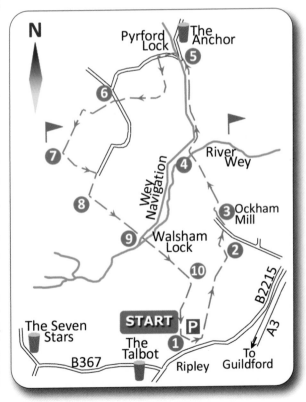

4 The path reaches the **River Wey** on your left-hand side. Keep following the path over a high wooden bridge and after 50 metres you will see the **Wey**

Navigation Canal in front of you. Turn right onto the towpath and follow the path all the way alongside the canal until you reach **Pyrford Lock** and the **Anchor pub**.

5 Turn left over the lock (as you are facing the Anchor) and walk along **Lock Lane** for 150 metres. Just as you see **Pyrford Marina** on your right, turn left onto a footpath at the fingerpost. Follow the yellow waymarkers across **Pyrford golf course**, straight ahead and then right past a small water feature and, keeping the feature on your right, turn right towards the houses ahead of you. Join a clay track and walk over a small grassed area, and then through a gate into a field. Keeping the fence on your right, cross the field, and exit through another gate.

6 Cross **Lock Lane** to your right and follow the bridleway sign. At the end of the driveway, go over the stile and follow the footpath around the edge of the field. As you reach the electricity pylon, turn left onto another footpath and follow this path over another junction. At the next junction, just as the electricity cables are above you, take the footpath to the left.

7 Follow this path down to the road and turn right onto the road.

8 After 250 metres, turn left, following the public footpath sign through a green gate down a private lane. You will have woods on your right and a golf course on your left. At the end of the lane you reach **Walsham Lock and Gates** and you can hear the crashing sound of the water as it rushes through the weir.

9 Bear left to cross the canal, then right past the lock-keeper's house and then left again over the weir. Do beware of the fast-running water. Keep straight ahead on the footpath, following this over a small bridge and through some fields. After a second bridge, keep left on the bridleway, ignoring the footpath to your right.

10 At the end of the pathway you will arrive at **Ripley Green**. Cross a small lane and turn right onto the green, following the footpath so that you are walking parallel to the lane. Follow this path all the way back along the green to where you have parked.

Whitmoor Common

Meg at Whitmoor Common.

A lovely, safe, circular walk, that takes you around Whitmoor Common, the largest expanse of open heathland in the Guildford area. The common contains areas of both wet and dry heathland and the walk takes you across some boardwalks past a house in which Lloyd George lived for a time. You will enjoy a range of scenery, with the walk starting on the flat heathland, winding through gorse and heather and then taking you through copses of mixed pine and silver birch trees.

Dogs can run free for the whole walk (unless you take the diversion to the pub!) and there is plenty to explore, with trees, streams, gorse and heathland. You will also undoubtedly meet other dog walkers on the common and as per normal end up with new friends.

Terrain
The footpaths are mainly sandy, except in the wetland areas where you follow a well-maintained boardwalk. The bridleway halfway round the walk can be muddy. There is only one short hill to climb so the going is generally easy.

Where to park
The Salt Box Road car park. **OS map:** Explorer 145 (GR SU 983530).

How to get there
Salt Box Road runs between the A320 and the A322 north of Guildford. From the A3 heading south, turn off for Burpham and take the A3100, Clay Lane, through Jacobs Well. At the A320, turn left and then first right. Follow this road down under a railway line and the car park is ½ mile on your right. Heading north on the A3, turn off on the A322 and take the right turn along Salt Box Road after about 2 miles, to reach the car park on the left.

Nearest refreshments
The **Jolly Farmer** in Burdenshot Road, just off the walk route at point 4, serves a range of pub food, including game, and has a garden for the summer months. Dogs are allowed on the tiled areas of the bar. ☎ 01483 234658; www.jollyfarmerworplesdon.co.uk

The Walk
. . . .

1 From the car park, with your back to the road, take the path marked by the waymarker to your right that runs adjacent to the road, taking you through some woods. After 200 metres, head straight across the footpath crossroads. As you continue you should have a field on your right that may contain horses. Keep right where the path joins the main bridleway.

Dog factors
. . . .
Distance: 3 miles.
Road walking: 100 metres along a private driveway if you take the diversion to the pub.
Livestock: None.
Stiles: None.
Nearest vets: Alder Veterinary Practice, Guildford.

2 When you enter a small grassy area, turn sharp left onto the common and follow the sandy path through the gorse and heather. Where the path bears to the left after 100 metres, go straight on down a narrow sandy path between the gorse bushes. Keep on this path. You will reach the boardwalk after 200 metres – take this through the wetland area.

3 At the end of the boardwalk, cross over a small wooden bridge back into the woods and then turn right. Follow this footpath through the woods and you will reach a big white house that was once lived in by Lloyd George. Keeping this on your right, walk past the house and down the gravel driveway.

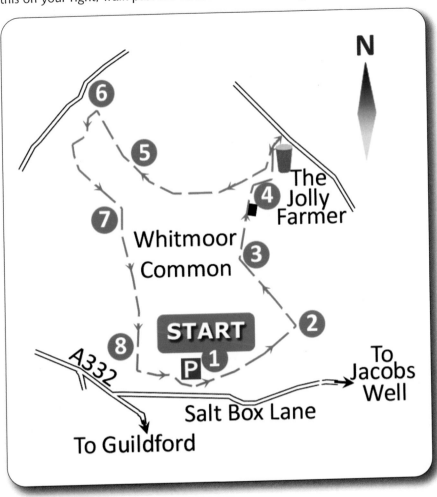

4 As you reach the tarmac lane, *turn right to reach the **Jolly Farmer pub***, which is 200 metres down the lane. Bear right across a common green area and across a car park – the pub is on your right. *If you don't want to divert to the pub*, turn left onto the tarmac drive and follow this until you reach **Whitmoor Hatch House**. Turn right onto a public bridleway. Keep on this footpath, until you reach the top of the hill.

5 At the broken tarmac drive, turn left onto the drive, which bears round to the right. In 20 metres after the right turn, turn left onto a track in the woods. Follow this path for a short way through the woods and into the open heather. Keeping a small hedge on your right, walk up the hill to a bench underneath a large oak tree where you can enjoy a good view of the common.

6 Keeping the bench behind you, take the footpath to the left ahead of you, following the marker sign towards the woods. At the woods, turn left and follow the path downhill along a sandy track with a private house on your right.

7 At the bridleway at the bottom of the hill, turn right past a small dewpond, and then left onto a footpath signposted to the car park. After 400 metres, you pass another dewpond and cross a wooden footbridge over a stream. Keep right.

8 As you leave the woodland, take a left-hand footpath (not marked) up past a metal cattle trough on your right. Follow the path round to the right through the trees. At the top of the hill turn left onto a bridleway and then go right through the woods towards the road. Where the path branches, turn left onto a path that leads you back to the car park.

Horsell Common

The McLaren Technology Park.

I call this walk my technology walk, as it incorporates Horsell Common which H.G. Wells used as the landing point for his Martians in *The War of the Worlds*, with its sand pit and majestic, brooding pines. From there you walk across the McLaren Technology Park, past the iconic McLaren headquarters building and then across one end of Fairoaks airport where you might need to duck as the planes land and take off over your head! You then circle back through some woods to re-enter Horsell Common.

The common is a popular dog-walking area and your dogs are bound to sniff out some friends, as well as enjoying a bit of squirrel chasing in the woods. There are plenty of water holes and streams for dipping in, and the newly-landscaped technology park with its pond and wetland areas is interesting to see.

Terrain

The walk across the common is flat and over a range of paths, including some sandy bridleways. Across the technology park, the path is well laid with some hardcore, and finally through the airfield and woods there is a mixture of grass and leafy tracks. The path on the return past the airfield can get boggy.

Where to park

The Six Cross Roads car park on the A245, Shores Road. **OS map:** Explorer 160 (GR TQ 013604).

How to get there

From junction 11 of the M25, take the turning west towards Woking. Turn left onto the A320 at the large roundabout and then drive straight over the next two roundabouts. At the third, turn right onto the A245 and the car park is 200 metres on your right.

Nearest refreshments

Drive back to Ottershaw to the **Castle**, where dogs are allowed in the Castle Bar and in the garden. A good selection of pub food is available. ☎ 01932 872373; www.the-castle-ottershaw.co.uk

The Walk

● ●

1 From the car park, with the road behind you, take the footpath at the far left-hand end of the car park. This leads up to a 'Looking after the Future' sign. Keeping the sign on your left, follow the footpath through the trees, all the time walking away from the car park. Keep following this footpath, ignoring any other paths. You will pass a wooden bench on your right.

2 This path will bring you out at the sand pit, where H. G. Wells' Martians landed and there will be a 'Y'-shaped tree in front of you, with a bench to the right of it. Turn right here and follow the path round the edge of the sand pit. After 50 metres the path goes down into the sandpit. Walk diagonally across the pit to the left, keeping the water on your left. You will have the sandy 'beach' ahead of you and to your right as you cross.

Dog factors

● ●

Distance: 4½ miles.
Road walking: 100 metres along Chertsey Road on exiting and entering the airport section.
Livestock: There could be cattle in the field at point 8.
Stiles: None.
Nearest vets: Vets4Pets, Woking.

Surrey – A Dog Walker's Guide

3 At the corner, exit the pit and you will be on a wide bridlepath. Turn right onto this path, which leads through the trees. You will have open heathland on your left.

4 About 100 metres before the road, just before an old gate, turn left following the footpath along the edge of the woods and heathland. You will still have the heathland on your left. Ignoring any side paths, follow this path through the woods and after 200 metres, just as the path bears left, take the right-hand path. After 50 metres you will reach an unmade road. Turn left and walk towards the cottage at the end. Take the footpath to the right of the cottage. You will now be in the **McLaren Technology Park** and the well-marked footpath bears left and winds around their

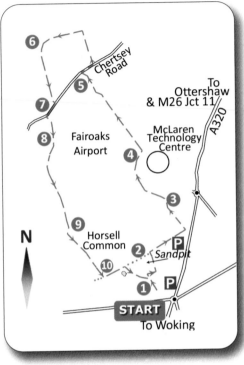

iconic centre past some restored wetland ponds. At the end of the park, turn left just before a green shed, over a small bridge and stream and keep straight on into the woods. As you exit the woods you come out onto the edge of **Fairoaks runway** – beware low-flying planes. Walk straight across the edge of the airfield and onto a small driveway, past some houses on your right.

5 As you reach the road, turn right, walk along the verge and after 100 metres, cross over to the footpath sign. Follow this footpath through the woods, with the field on your left-hand side. At the end of the field, turn left at the bridleway sign, so you continue to follow the edge of the field.

6 Keep straight on as you reach a public footpath sign, following the fence of the house on the left. You will reach a private lane; keep straight on following the bridleway link sign.

7 At the end of the lane, turn right onto the main road again and after 150 metres, cross over into the entrance to **Fairoaks Airport**. Walk up the road into the airport, keeping to the right.

8 After 150 metres, take the footpath to the right behind the airport buildings. You will pass the other end of the runway and pass over a small wooden bridge back over onto the common. You will have a hedge on your left. After 400 metres cross a second bridge and stream. Follow the restored bridleway into the trees.

9 At a house, bear left over another small bridge and then immediately right before you reach the house down a footpath through the trees which leads down alongside the edge of a field on your left. After 200 metres you will reach an unmade road; cross straight over onto a footpath through the trees. After 50 metres cross over another footpath and keep straight on as the slightly sunken footpath winds between gorse bushes and coppiced trees, with open heathland on your right. Ignore any small side paths. After 200 metres you will exit onto the heathland and there will be a pond on your left-hand side. Take the footpath to the far right of the pond as you face it, which follows the edge of the heathland along a coppiced hedge on your right. This path leads slightly uphill into the woods again and then downhill into the pine trees. Ignore any side paths.

10 After 300 metres, you will reach a wide bridle path. Turn left and follow the path through the avenue of pine trees. You will be able to see open heathland on your left and right. After 200 metres you will pass **Danewell Pond** on your right and just past this, as you start to walk uphill again, turn right at a large oak tree, keeping the pond and its clearing on your right-hand side. As you reach the end of the pond clearing, bear left uphill at a large old pine tree and keep straight ahead, ignoring a left-hand turning. Walk straight across a small clearing in the woods and after 75 metres turn left at the T-junction onto the path which you took from the car park. Follow this path back past the wooden bench and the information sign to the car park.

The sand pit on Horsell Common.

Chertsey Meads & Wey Meadows

The canal at Weybridge Lock.

Chertsey Meads is a council-owned public space lying between the River Thames and the River Bourne. Just over half of the Meads are designated as a local nature reserve and they are managed as hay meadows with wild flowers, birds and insects being found in abundance throughout the spring and summer. As so much of Surrey's unimproved grassland has been lost over the past 35 years, this area is now managed to ensure its preservation for future generations. This walk also takes in Wey Meadows on the banks of the River Wey and parts of the Wey Navigation Canal. There is a pub just over halfway round for some refreshment, or why not take a picnic and sit by the River Thames at the end of the walk?

The Meads are a popular dog-walking area, and your dogs will enjoy making new friends at the start and finish of this walk. There is plenty of water for swimming, although care should be taken near the canals and locks.

Terrain
A flat walk with dry towpaths, although in the winter months the Meads and field paths can get muddy.

Where to park
Park in the first car park on the left as you enter the Meads. **OS map:** Explorer 160 (GR TQ 054662).

How to get there
From junction 11 of the M25, take the A317 towards Addlestone. Turn left at the roundabout and then bear right at the next junction. After 200 metres, turn right down Mead Lane to the Meads.

Nearest refreshments
The **Pelican**, halfway round the walk, serves traditional pub food and has a garden overlooking the canal where you can sit and watch the boats go past. ☎ 01932 847956; www.pelicanaddlestone.co.uk

Or take a picnic and enjoy the views of the Thames from one of the picnic sites along the river after you return from your walk.

The Walk

❶ From the car park, cross the entrance road and take the footpath across the grass towards the willows and pylons. As you reach the opposite side of the fields, turn left, following the boundary of the field and the course of the **River Bourne**. You will see some large willow trees on your right. Continue on this path.

Dog factors

Distance: 5 miles.
Road walking: 500 metres down the quiet Wey Meadows private road and through the mobile home park.
Livestock: There may be livestock in the field beyond the River Bourne.
Stiles: 2.
Nearest vets: Donald Kingsnorth Associates, Chertsey.

2 At the third pylon turn right and cross a bridge over the River Bourne, which has dog swimming access. Go left over a stile into a field and then right so that you are walking away from the river. Follow this path through the field and eventually you will see a mobile home park on your right and a muddy pond on your left.

3 Some 100 metres after the start of the park, turn left across the field, following the footpath sign.

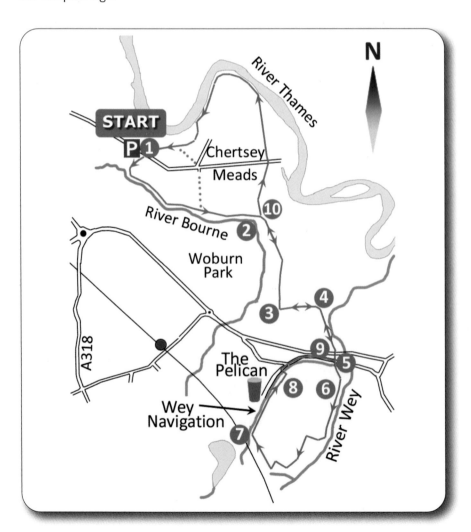

4 At the end of the field, climb over the stile and walk through a short stretch of overgrown brambles until you reach a road. Turn right onto the road and after 50 metres, cross the road and go through the woods onto the towpath of the **Wey Navigation**.

5 Follow the towpath, enjoying the views of the large houses that back onto the navigation, until you reach a bridge. Pass under the bridge where the **River Wey** and the canal join, and continue round to the right; this brings you up onto a road. Cross the road and the bridge, and take the lane to the left signposted to **Wey Meadows**. To your right is **Weybridge Town Lock**.

6 Walk down this private road through Wey Meadows, with the River Wey with its wildfowl on your left, until you reach a mobile home park. Enter the park and turn left and then right down the lane signposted Nos 25–40. At the end of that lane, pass straight through a gate into some woods.

7 After 200 metres this path brings you out onto the **Wey Navigation towpath** again. Turn right and follow the footpath along. On the opposite side of the canal are mooring points for canal boats, which are all painted different colours. Eventually, you will see the **Pelican pub** on the left-hand side of the canal.

8 At the bridge, turn left over it. *If you want to go to the **Pelican**, turn left again and follow the path back along the canal to the pub. If you don't, turn right and keep following the canal, albeit on the opposite side now. You are on a narrow raised path between the road and the canal.*

9 When you reach **Weybridge Town Lock** again, retrace your steps back along the towpath, then cross the road and go over the stiles and across the stream to the **Meads**.

10 On crossing the stream, keep straight ahead with the boundary on your right. Cross over a small lane, and eventually you will reach the **River Thames**. Turn left, following the path of the Thames back towards the car park.

Swinley Forest to Rapley Lake

Rapley Lake.

Swinley Forest, part of the Crown Estate, is situated just north of Bagshot. With its wide grassy avenues, towering trees and bubbling streams it is a magnificent destination for a walk. At the heart of the forest is Rapley Lake (although technically in Berkshire), which is surrounded by rhododendrons – giving a tremendous floral display in the spring. The forest edges the Bagshot Park estate, home of the Duke and Duchess of Wessex, so you never know who you might see across the fence! This is a walk for all seasons as the changing colours and shapes of the trees give the forest a different look as the year progresses.

These woods are simply doggie heaven: water, both in streams and ponds, trees, mud and other dog walkers all combine to ensure that they will have the time of their lives.

Terrain

A flat walk. Because of the nature of the ground and the preponderance of small streams, be prepared for some muddy patches.

Where to park

Vicarage Road, Bagshot, making sure that you don't block any other road users or residents. **OS map:** Explorer 160 (GR SU 905632).

How to get there

From the A30 through Bagshot, turn off along Church Road, drive past the church and then turn right into Vicarage Road. Drive to the end and park on your right.

Nearest refreshments

The **Three Mariners** in the centre of Bagshot serves a traditional range of pub dishes and welcomes dogs in all areas. You need to park on the street outside and watch out for the parking restrictions. ☎ 01276 473768; www.thethreemariners.co.uk

Alternatively, you can drive back up the A30 and turn right down School Road to the **Half Moon** at Windlesham, which serves great home-made food and local ales. Well-behaved dogs are allowed in the bar. ☎ 01276 473329; www.thehalfmoonwindlesham.com

The Walk

. . . .

1 From where you have parked, follow **Vicarage Road** down towards the un-made-up area. Turn right before the barrier through a kissing gate and then right again, following the footpath down to the end, where it turns left into the woods. This is a narrow path that takes you along the back of the houses. Keep following this path as it turns left and follows the edge of a field on your right. After a while it becomes a wide grassy track with magnificent trees on either side.

Dog factors

. . . .

Distance: 3 miles,
Road walking: None.
Livestock: None.
Stiles: None.
Nearest vets: Windlebrook Veterinary Clinic, Bagshot.

2 After 250 metres on this wide path, turn right down another wide grassy path. At the end of this path there is a grassy bank with a tree trunk set in it; walk past this and keep straight on through the trees and rhododendrons, ignoring any footpaths to the left or right. At the T-junction at the end, turn left. You should have a lovely little clear stream on your right-hand side, as well as some large rhododendron bushes. Follow the path along the stream. It will cross over the stream to the right and, keeping on the footpath, you will reach the edge of the woods. In front of you is **Bagshot Park**, home of the Duke and Duchess of Wessex.

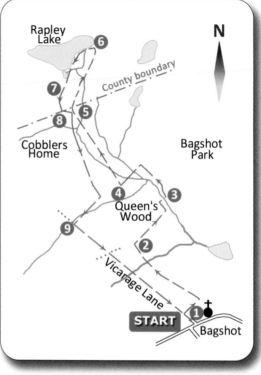

3 Turn left, following the edge of the woods, with the grounds of Bagshot Park on your right. As you reach the next wide grassy avenue, turn left and follow this avenue downhill.

4 On reaching the bottom of the hill, take the footpath to your right; this leads over a small stream and winds gently through the woods – you will find a couple of good dog swimming areas along here. After 300 metres, the path widens to another grassy avenue; keep following this route between the trees. As you leave the main woods into an area of bracken, there is a big footpath crossroads with a fingerpost. Take the right-hand path, ignoring the fingerpost. This path marks the county boundary with Berkshire!

5 Follow this path through the woods across another small stream and at the top of the path you will reach a 'no public access' sign and an unmade gravel road.

6 Turn left onto the path and **Rapley Lake** is on your right-hand side. It is surrounded by trees and you can enjoy the reflections in the still water as you take the path round the lake. Depending on the time of year you will also see a selection of waterfowl. Follow this path along the side of the lake; you will arrive at a bridge that crosses an outlet from the lake, no doubt feeding all those streams.

7 Some 200 metres after the bridge, turn left down a grassy track leading you back into the woods. You will pass through some old metal gates and eventually arrive back at the large cross path junction with the fingerpost you saw at the end of point 4.

8 Turn right, following the only footpath you have not been on. Follow this path through the trees, ignoring the left-hand turn. At the next big crossway, turn right onto another of the wide grassy avenues.

9 At the end of the avenue, pass through the gate and turn left. You are now on **Vicarage Lane** with woods on your left and right. Follow this bridleway all the way back to reach your car in **Vicarage Road**.

In Swinley Forest.

APPENDIX

The following are veterinary practices that are close to the walks described:

Alder Veterinary Practice
137 Worplesdon Road,
Guildford, GU2 9XA
☎ 01483 536036

Ash Barn Veterinary Surgery
Unit 5, Ockley Court Farm,
Coles Lane, Ockley, RH5 5LS
☎ 01306 713177

Banstead Village Vets
170a High Street, Banstead
SM7 2NZ
☎ 01737 210011

Brelades Vets
Rothwell House, Church Road,
Bookham, KT23 3JP
☎ 01372 452531
and
Station Road, Gomshall, GU5 9LE
☎ 01483 205066

Cobham Veterinary Centre
Byfleet Road, Cobham, KT11 1DS
☎ 01932 868786

Denbies View Veterinary Centre
Westcott Road, Dorking, RH4 3DP
☎ 01306 882996

Donald Kingsnorth Associates
6 London Street, Chertsey, KT16 8AA
☎ 01932 567789

Elstead Veterinary Surgery
The Green, Elstead, GU8 6DD
☎ 01252 703412

Gayton Veterinary Clinic
7 South Parade, Horley Row,
Horley, RH6 8BH
☎ 01293 771560

Medivet Esher
20 Manor Road, North
Hinchley Wood, KT10 0SH
☎ 0208 398 8005

Priory Vets
10 Evesham Road, Reigate,
RH2 9DF
☎ 01737 242190

Tanhouse Veterinary Clinic
1 Tanhouse Road, Broadham Green,
Old Oxted, RH8 9EP
☎ 01883 722771

Vets4Pets
Inside Pets at Home, Lion Retail Park,
Oriental Road, Woking, GU22 8BD
☎ 01483 815104

Village Veterinary Centre
Thornton Side, Watercolour,
Merstham, RH1 2NP
☎ 01737 646212

Windlebrook Veterinary Clinic
46 High Street, Bagshot, GU19 5AW
☎ 01276 473516

Winton Lodge Vets
36 Ashley Road, Epsom, KT18 5BH
☎ 01372 722313

Yew Tree Veterinary Centre
Horsham Road, Cranleigh, GU6 8DP
☎ 01483 275665